Tailored resources for better grades

MAKE THE GRADE

WJEC GCSE

English and English Language

Natalie Simpson

Consultant: **Stuart Sage**

Higher

Revision Workbook

www.pearsonschoolsandfecolleges.co.uk

✓ Free online support
✓ Useful weblinks
✓ 24 hour online ordering

0845 630 33 33

Heinemann

Part of Pearson

Heinemann is an imprint of Pearson Education Limited, a company incorporated in England and Wales, having its registered office at Edinburgh Gate, Harlow, Essex, CM20 2JE. Registered company number: 872828

www.pearsonschoolsandfecolleges.co.uk

Heinemann is the registered trademark of Pearson Education Limited

Text © Pearson Education Limited 2011

First published 2011

15 14 13 12 11
10 9 8 7 6 5 4 3 2 1

British Library Cataloguing in Publication Data
A catalogue record for this book is available from the British Library on request.

ISBN 978 0 435 02756 8

Edited by Julia Naughton
Designed and produced by Kamae Design, Oxford
Cover design by Wooden Ark Studios, Leeds
Picture research by Elena Wright
Cover photo © Gaertner/Alamy
Printed in Spain by Grafos, Barcelona

Acknowledgements
The authors and publisher would like to thank the following individuals and organisations for permission to reproduce material in this book:

P7 short extract from Teens' Speech produced by Barnardos. Reprinted with kind permissions. P8 'Hilton Maldives Iru Fushi Resort and Spa' extract from www.thomson.co.uk. Reprinted with kind permission of Thomson. This text belongs to Thomson and must not be included anywhere else without prior written permission. P19 Cover from 'Driven to Distraction' by Jeremy Clarkson, published by Penguin Books. Reprinted with kind permission of Penguin Books UK. P19 'Driven to Distraction' by Jeremy Clarkson review by Liz Hunt, The Telegraph, 9th October 2009 © Telegraph Media Group Limited. P27 'Go Ape' extract, reprinted with kind permission. www.goape.co.uk. P34 cover and blurb from 'Chris Hoy: The Autobiography' published by HarperCollins Publishers. Reprinted with kind permission of the publisher. P36 'Save yourself more than just a packet…' article, adapted from www.nhs.uk/Livewell/smoking/Pages/Teensmokersquit.aspx. Material adapted from content first published by the Department of Health (NHS Choices – nhs.uk). Reprinted with kind permission. P46 'Apple iPhone 4 Review' adapted from www.mobile-phones-uk.org.uk/apple-iphone-4.htm. Reprinted with permission of Landmark Internet. P85 'Diggerland' text taken from www.diggerland.com. Reprinted with kind permission. P86 'Bowland Wild Boar Park' text taken from www.wildboarpark.co.uk. Reprinted with kind permission. P110 'Back to basics: choosing a mobile phone' by Clive Woodyear, Sunday Times, 8 March 2010. Reprinted with permission.

The publisher would like to thank the following for their kind permission to reproduce their photographs:

Piii Shutterstock.com: Nagel Photography; PPiv-v Shutterstock.com: Nagel Photography; PPvi-vii Shutterstock.com: Nagel Photography; P2 Shutterstock.com: Nagel Photography; P4 Shutterstock.com: sergeyDV; P10 Shutterstock.com: Nagel Photography; P11 John Byford; P13 Shutterstock.com: Gail Johnston; P16 Shutterstock.com: Nagel Photography; P17 Pearson Education Ltd: Martin Bedall; P24 Shutterstock.com: Nagel Photography; P27 Shutterstock.com: Fotum; P32 Shutterstock.com: Nagel Photography; P35 Getty Images: Pierre Bourrier; P36 Getty Images: Caroline Purser; P40 Shutterstock.com: Nagel Photography; P42 Blend: Plush Studios / TIPS Images; P46 Getty Images; PP48-49 Shutterstock.com: Nagel Photography; P50 Shutterstock.com: Nagel Photography; P51 Getty Images: Jamie Grill; P56 Shutterstock.com: Nagel Photography; P59 Alamy Images: dbimages; P64 Shutterstock.com: Nagel Photography; P69 Getty Images: Ms Harriet Evans; P72 Shutterstock.com: Nagel Photography; P80 Shutterstock.com: Nagel Photography; P82 Getty Images: Image source; P88 Shutterstock.com: Nagel Photography; P91 Masterfile UK Ltd: Andrew Olney; P96 Shutterstock.com: Nagel Photography; P106 Shutterstock.com: Nagel Photography.

All other images © Pearson Education Limited

Every effort has been made to contact copyright holders of material reproduced in this book. Any omissions will be rectified in subsequent printings if notice is given to the publishers.

Contents

Introduction

This Workbook is designed to help you focus your revision and improve your grade in WJEC GCSE English and English Language.

Some students think that there is no need to revise for English and English Language. This is simply not true! You can do things to improve your chances of getting a good grade and you can revise for English and English Language as much as for any of your other subjects.

The more you revise and practise past paper questions, the more confident you will become in knowing just what the examiner is looking for. By making yourself familiar with the type of questions being asked and the mark schemes used by the examiner, you will increase your chances of getting a higher grade.

How to improve your revision techniques

1 The first thing to do is to make use of your own teacher, as they are a very valuable resource! Listen carefully to all the revision and tips your teacher gives you in lesson time. If there is something you are unsure about, remember to ask. Your teacher may hold extra revision classes at lunchtime in the run-up to the exam sessions. If so, make sure you take advantage of this opportunity.

2 Check that you are familiar with what the exam papers look like, how many marks are awarded to each question and how much you will be expected to write in your answer booklet.

3 When you are ready to revise, find a quiet area away from any distractions like noise or television. Remember to take regular breaks and pace yourself. It is difficult to concentrate for very long periods of time. Breaking your revision into manageable sessions is much more worthwhile and you will remember more in the long run.

4 Use a checklist like the Revision Planner on page 2 in this Workbook. This could be a useful starting point for you to find out exactly what you know already, and to help you find any gaps in your knowledge.

5 The most effective way to revise is through active strategies. This means:

▶ practising the skills you have studied

▶ taking part in completing revision activities

▶ comparing your answers with sample answers to see where you can improve your performance.

When you practise answering past paper questions, always to time yourself. This will help you to understand what it will feel like to be under pressure when you are writing in the exam itself.

6 Finally, be positive: think about what you *can* do, not what you can't. Good luck!

Revision checklist

How confident do you feel about each of the areas below that you need to revise for your exam?

Fill in the revision checklist below.

▶ Tick green if you feel confident about this topic.

▶ Tick amber if you know some things, but revision will help improve your knowledge and skills to the best they can be.

▶ Tick red if you are not confident about two or more aspects of this topic.

There will be a chance to fill in this table after your revision and before your exam, to see how much progress you have made during your revision.

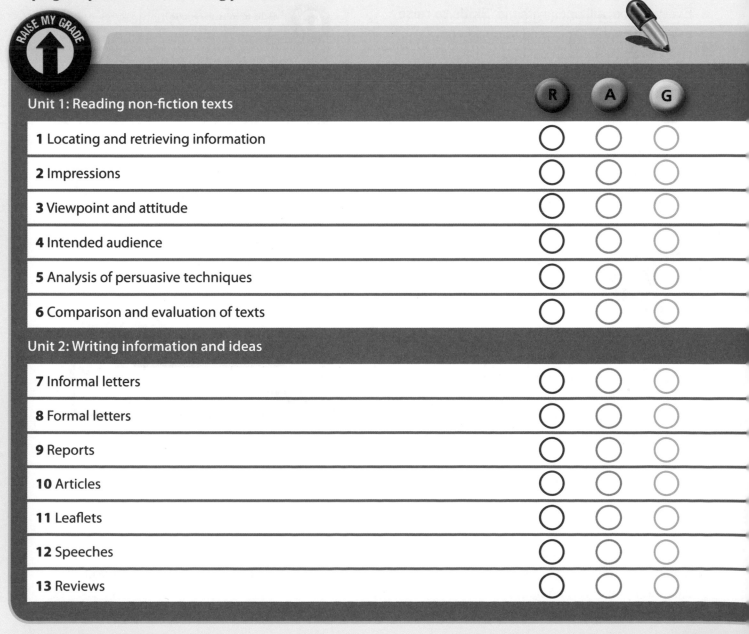

	R	A	G
Unit 1: Reading non-fiction texts			
1 Locating and retrieving information	○	○	○
2 Impressions	○	○	○
3 Viewpoint and attitude	○	○	○
4 Intended audience	○	○	○
5 Analysis of persuasive techniques	○	○	○
6 Comparison and evaluation of texts	○	○	○
Unit 2: Writing information and ideas			
7 Informal letters	○	○	○
8 Formal letters	○	○	○
9 Reports	○	○	○
10 Articles	○	○	○
11 Leaflets	○	○	○
12 Speeches	○	○	○
13 Reviews	○	○	○

Using the WJEC GCSE English and English Language Revision Workbook

The WJEC GCSE English and English Language Student Workbook has been written to help you to revise the skills and knowledge that you will have covered in your GCSE English/English Language course over Year 10 and Year 11.

The Workbook has been designed for you to revise **actively**. There is room for you to write answers to activities and practise exam questions, though in some cases you will need to continue your answer on a separate sheet of paper. The **'Extra paper'** icon will indicate where this is necessary. You are encouraged to highlight and annotate exam questions and texts as you will in the exam.

Every lesson will open with the **'Skills to raise my grade'** table. You need to decide how confident you are with each of the skills listed. You can record your confidence using a traffic-light system. The lesson then goes over these skills and at the end of the lesson you review your confidence. Hopefully your knowledge of the skills will have improved.

Each activity suggests how much time you should spend on it. This is for guidance only. Where you answer an exam question the timings will be linked to how much time you will have in the exam to answer this type of question.

Each lesson has a **'Raise my grade'** activity. In these activities you will practise the specific skills that you have revised in the lesson, and try to improve a lower grade answer by one grade. This is the Higher Tier Workbook, so you will be focusing on C–A* grades.

At the end of each lesson there is a **'GradeStudio'** section. This is to give you an opportunity to read examiner comments and mark schemes, and to match these to example student answers. This exam work should help you understand the mark scheme and how to get the highest grade you are capable of.

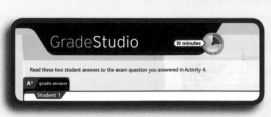

You can find answers to the Workbook activities online at www.pearsonschools.co.uk/gcse2010/wjecenglish Click on Free Resources and open the Higher answer file.

Good luck with your revision. Remember – you still have time to improve your performance in the exam by at least a grade.

In the exam room, remember to be confident, take a deep breath and don't panic! Read all the questions carefully and put into practice all the advice from your teacher and the helpful hints you will find in this Workbook.

Reading mark scheme

Grade descriptions

A* grade answer
(9–10 marks)

- thorough, purposeful and perceptive response
- skilfully selected range of ideas and evidence
- covers a range of different points
- assured grasp of the text
- clarity of understanding
- totally focused on the question

A grade answer
(8 marks)

- thorough and detailed response
- range of different ideas and evidence
- covers a range of different points
- assured grasp of the text
- focused, relevant and detailed

B grade answer
(7 marks)

- a clear response with a competent level of detail
- selects a range of appropriate material
- explores a number of valid ideas
- clear focus on the question

C grade answer
(5–6 marks)

- a clear response
- selects appropriate detail from the text
- shows understanding of the key areas in the text
- the answer will have a clear understanding of the question

D grade answer
(3–4 marks)

- makes simple comments about the text
- some focus on the question
- will include some appropriate detail from the text

E grade answer
(2 marks)

- some comments about surface features of the text
- some focus on the question
- some details from the text

Skills you need ▶

You must show that you can:
- recognise location/retrieval questions
- organise an answer
- develop and demonstrate location/retrieval skills

Skills to raise my grade

Fill in the RAG table below to show how confident you are in the following areas:	R	A	G
I can read and understand questions that are asking me to find information in a text.	○	○	○
I am able to scan through a text quickly or read it thoroughly to help me locate different pieces of relevant information.	○	○	○
I can select the correct information to answer an exam question successfully.	○	○	○
I can organise my answer chronologically and clearly.	○	○	○

Locating or finding information in a text might seem like a straightforward task, but there are a number of skills that can help you increase your marks.

In this lesson you will learn some useful key words that will help you in the examination.

You will think about how to organise an answer and you will practise locating information in a number of different activities. Finally, this lesson will help you focus on your own answers and how to improve them.

4 minutes

Activity 1

1 Write definitions for each of the following key words.

Key words	Definitions
Locate	
Retrieve	
Track	
Chronological	

4 minutes

Activity 2

Tick the questions where you think you are *only* being asked to locate information.

a List ten reasons why schools should recycle. ☐

b What evidence does the writer use to make it clear to the reader that theft is wrong? ☐

c Find any information in the text that you think supports a change in the legal age for driving. ☐

d What benefits does exercise have on the body? ☐

e Why did Heather give up smoking? ☐

It is vital that you check how many marks each question is worth before you begin your answer. Looking at the marks is a good guide to how many points/ideas you need to include.

Remember: never copy out huge chunks of text – carefully select the information and, where relevant, put it into your own words.

Writing chronologically helps you to track exactly where you are up to when locating information in a passage and writing your answer. A chronological answer also helps the examiner follow your answer more easily when they are marking your work.

10 minutes

Activity 3

This student was asked to read a text about Ben Fogle and to list his achievements. See if you can reorganise their answer in a more helpful order by adding a number to each of the boxes. There is no source text provided; what you need to focus on here is the order of the answer.

☐ Before his TV career began, Ben Fogle worked for *Tatler* magazine.

☐ In 2008 he took part in the World Coal Carrying Championships, finishing 22nd.

☐ With James Cracknell, Fogle was first to finish in the 2005-2006 Atlantic Rowing Race, completing the 3000 mile race.

☐ In 2004 he completed the six-day Marathon des Sables across 160 miles (260 km) of the Sahara Desert.

☐ In October 2009, Fogle and James Cracknell cycled a rickshaw 423 miles from Edinburgh to London non-stop.

☐ His team came 2nd in the 770km South Pole Race in February 2009.

☐ His first TV role was in the reality show Castaway, in 2000.

☐ Having completed his marathon Atlantic rowing race, his first book Offshore was published by Penguin in 2006.

☐ Fogle currently writes a weekly Country Diary for the Sunday Telegraph.

☐ Fogle was awarded an honorary doctorate by the University of Portsmouth in 2007.

This is what an examiner said about the answer above.

Examiner comment

This candidate would not be penalised for including all of the correct points, but writing in this erratic style often means that you miss out vital information and do not give a good overall impression of your organisational skills.

12 minutes

Activity 4

Read this leaflet from *Futuristic Living*.

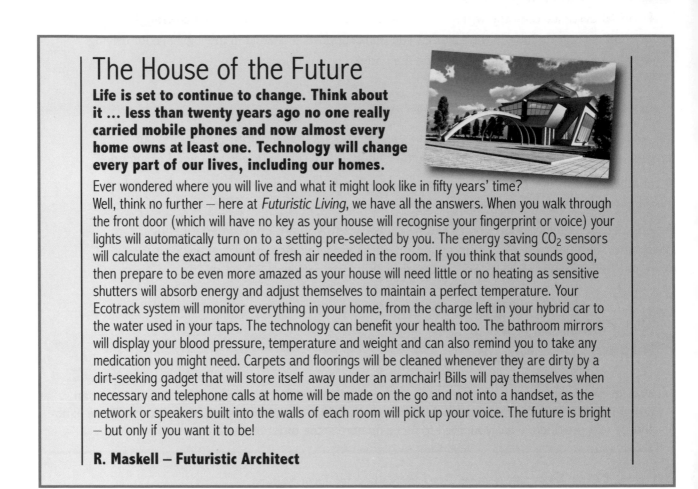

The House of the Future

Life is set to continue to change. Think about it ... less than twenty years ago no one really carried mobile phones and now almost every home owns at least one. Technology will change every part of our lives, including our homes.

Ever wondered where you will live and what it might look like in fifty years' time? Well, think no further — here at *Futuristic Living*, we have all the answers. When you walk through the front door (which will have no key as your house will recognise your fingerprint or voice) your lights will automatically turn on to a setting pre-selected by you. The energy saving CO_2 sensors will calculate the exact amount of fresh air needed in the room. If you think that sounds good, then prepare to be even more amazed as your house will need little or no heating as sensitive shutters will absorb energy and adjust themselves to maintain a perfect temperature. Your Ecotrack system will monitor everything in your home, from the charge left in your hybrid car to the water used in your taps. The technology can benefit your health too. The bathroom mirrors will display your blood pressure, temperature and weight and can also remind you to take any medication you might need. Carpets and floorings will be cleaned whenever they are dirty by a dirt-seeking gadget that will store itself away under an armchair! Bills will pay themselves when necessary and telephone calls at home will be made on the go and not into a handset, as the network or speakers built into the walls of each room will pick up your voice. The future is bright — but only if you want it to be!

R. Maskell — Futuristic Architect

It often helps to annotate the exam question as below, before you start to write your answer.

Put the information you locate into a paragraph

Only include information about the actual house

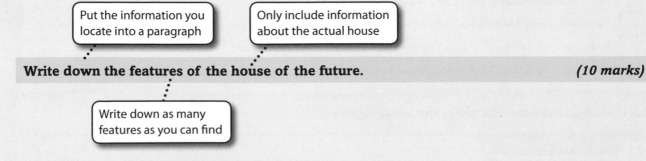

Write down the features of the house of the future. *(10 marks)*

Write down as many features as you can find

1 Track through the text methodically and highlight words/phrases that you will need in your answer.

2 Write up your answer in the writing space opposite, referring to the grade criteria on page vii.

_____

_____

_____

_____

_____

_____

_____

_____

_____

_____

Now look at the two student answers that follow and the comments that the examiner has made about them.

C grade answer

Student 1

The student has explained why this feature is useful, but this explanation does not gain any extra reward as the student was not asked to explain their ideas

The house of the future sounds pretty good and it has loads of features that most people would love to have in their own homes. I'm not sure that many of us will be living in houses like this anytime soon as it will probably cost loads. One of the features of the house are that the bathroom mirrors can check your health ✓ which would be really useful as you would know if there was anything wrong with you really quickly. The lights would be able to come on automatically as soon as you walked in ✓ and this would be good as it would make you feel really safe. Another good feature is that Carpets can be cleaned by themselves ✓ by a clever little machine and this will save the house cleaner (my mum) quite a lot of time. There will be no key (voice activation will open the door) ✓ and the temperature will adjust itself to suit you. ✓

The student has slipped into commentary and is not immediately focused on the question

Again, explanation not needed

Student finally grasps the technique in the end, but has wasted a lot of time

Examiner comment 1

The student has worked hard and written quite a lot of information. There are some areas that need work. The student has not worked through the article chronologically and therefore misses a good number of points. The student has spent an unnecessary amount of time explaining why the features are useful. This was not part of the task, so the student has wasted time as a result of not reading the task carefully. However, the technique does improve towards the end and the student has covered sufficient features to warrant a grade C overall.

A*   grade answer

Student 2

Neat overview to begin.

Future homes may not look very different compared to those we live in today but the features and technology will differ greatly. Homes will not be opened by a key ✓ but will be fingerprint or voice-activated. ✓ Another feature of the future house is that lights will automatically turn on ✓ and they will adjust to a pre-determined brightness. ✓ Energy sensors create the perfect mix of air ✓ and the temperature will be regulated by way of shutters. ✓ An Ecotrack system will be a major feature ✓ and the features of this advanced technology will not only check the power in your car ✓ but the water used in taps. ✓ Bathroom mirrors will be a great feature as they can calculate weight, blood pressure and body temperatures. ✓ One appealing feature is that floors will clean themselves. ✓ Telephone calls will be made at any point in the house as a handset will not be required. ✓

Examiner comment 2

The answer begins with a neat overview where the candidate succinctly summarises the article. Overall, the answer includes more information than is necessary but the information is clear and thorough. The student has worked through the passage in a chronological order and has tracked the relevant information. Ideas are nicely stacked together to limit the need for additional sentences. This answer would be awarded grade A*.

3   Review your own answer using the table below and see how it compares to the examples you have just read.

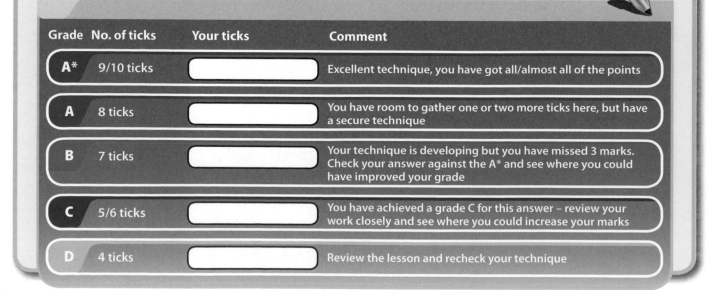

Grade	No. of ticks	Your ticks	Comment
A*	9/10 ticks		Excellent technique, you have got all/almost all of the points
A	8 ticks		You have room to gather one or two more ticks here, but have a secure technique
B	7 ticks		Your technique is developing but you have missed 3 marks. Check your answer against the A* and see where you could have improved your grade
C	5/6 ticks		You have achieved a grade C for this answer – review your work closely and see where you could increase your marks
D	4 ticks		Review the lesson and recheck your technique

10 minutes

Activity 5

The transcript below is taken from a video called 'Teens' Speech' by the Barnados charity. Read the transcript to help you think about the things that the teenagers are concerned about.

Leigh-Ann: I think the hardest thing about being a teenager in the family today is that you almost can't identify with your parents. I feel like that's the biggest breakdown of communication that you'll ever encounter.

Zoya: Teenagers have difficulty in sharing what they really actually feel, even with their friends as well. Not having a family and not being able to talk to them results in young people going into gangs so they have a sense of belonging.

Mary Jane: In my area, gangs are quite common because it's like different territories they claim them.

Bianca: I wouldn't be too surprised if one of my friends did carry a weapon because of the area I live in. If you grow up around violence, and you're exposed to it from a young age, then you accept it as the norm, and then you act it out because that is what's expected of you. And I think that's what so many young people do.

Katie: When I go to the shops and I see a group or gang, I feel intimidated that they're going to hurt me. Thoughts are going through my mind: do they have weapons? It's like they're controlling us, like: don't come near us or we'll hurt you. Like they don't have the right to do that.

Leigh-Ann: Great Britain is in a crisis right now. I mean, politicians are corrupt, finances are corrupt. Everywhere you look it's like, who do you trust?

Now that you have read the transcript, list the things that the teenagers are concerned about:

_____

_____

_____

_____

_____

_____

_____

Read the article on the Hilton Maldives Spa and the exam question below.

The writer tries to suggest that the villas in the Hilton Resort will be perfect for any guest. Find the evidence he uses to suggest this. *(10 marks)*

Hilton Maldives Iru Fushi Resort and Spa

'If you're looking for a stylish sanctuary, it has to be the Hilton Maldives.'

Location-wise, the Noonu Atoll is a real getaway – all sugar-white sands, bright blue waters and tropical greenery. And it's so off the beaten track, it's only reachable by seaplane. So if you're after that miles-from-anywhere feeling, the Resort is ideal.

On the accommodation front, there's a selection to choose from. You'll find a string of water villas dotting the ocean on stilts. And as you'd expect, the views from here are pretty special – think wide blue skies and endless water. Private sundecks and outdoor bathrooms offer up the best spots to enjoy them. As for other extras, Bose home theatre systems add a real touch of luxury. Back on dry land, you'll find a collection of beach villas nestled among the island's flora. These beach-hut inspired havens offer up airy rooms, whirlpool baths, and private terraces complete with over-sized daybeds. Décor-wise, all rooms are dressed in neutral colours, with chunky wooden furniture and big four-poster beds, creating a stylish-but-comfortable vibe. Flatscreen TVs and iPod connections add the finishing touches.

When you're ready for something a little more active, you'll find floodlit tennis courts and a PADI-approved dive centre. The waters surrounding the island are teeming with underwater life – think turtles, rays, and even dolphins – so there are some fantastic dives right on your doorstep.

On the food front, there's plenty on the menu to keep things interesting. Just-landed seafood plays a big part, while huge international buffets serve up everything from Oriental eats to Italian favourites. And there are plenty of places to eat and drink, too. We're talking six-course dinners under the stars, leisurely al fresco lunches on the beach, and sunset cocktails on the seafront.

Now look at this student's answer to the exam question and the examiner comments that were made. Annotate the student answer with your improvements, so that it achieves full marks.

> The writer tries to suggest that the villas will be perfect for any guest as they include a range of different pieces of evidence. The water villas sound perfect as they have superb 'views' of the wide blue skies and endless water. They also have private sundecks, outdoor bathrooms and Bose home theatre systems. The beach villas have also been advertised as perfect too and have the following features: whirlpool baths, private terraces and over-sized daybeds. So, overall the resort and the villas should appeal to most people who are looking to relax and enjoy their holiday.

Examiner comment

This answer would be awarded a grade B. Look at how the candidate neatly includes detail and uses short but relevant quotations. The candidate has only included 7 different points; to reach an A* and 10 marks, this answer needs to gather a little more evidence. Look at how the question only asks you to focus on the villas – make sure you read the question carefully as there is a great deal of irrelevant information in the passage.

RAISE MY GRADE

Skills to raise my grade

Now you have completed this lesson on locating and retrieving information, it's time to fill in the RAG table below to see if your confidence has improved.

	R	A	G
I can read and understand which questions are asking me to find information in a text.	○	○	○
I am able to scan through a text quickly or read it thoroughly to help me locate different pieces of relevant information.	○	○	○
I can select the correct information to answer an exam question.	○	○	○
I can organise my answer chronologically and coherently.	○	○	○

2 Impressions

Skills to raise my grade

RAISE MY GRADE ↑

Fill in the RAG table below to show how confident you are in the following areas:	R	A	G
I can read and understand which questions are asking me to give an impression of a text and its contents.	○	○	○
I can use a range of reading skills to understand the impressions a writer may create in a text and the way they are created.	○	○	○
I can select the correct information and add my own impression to answer an exam question.	○	○	○
I can organise my answer chronologically and coherently.	○	○	○

When you are answering questions about impressions, you need to read through a text while thinking about the impression you are given about a person, place, organisation or event at any given time.

In this lesson you will learn what to focus on in an impressions question, how to include evidence in your answer and how to improve your own answers.

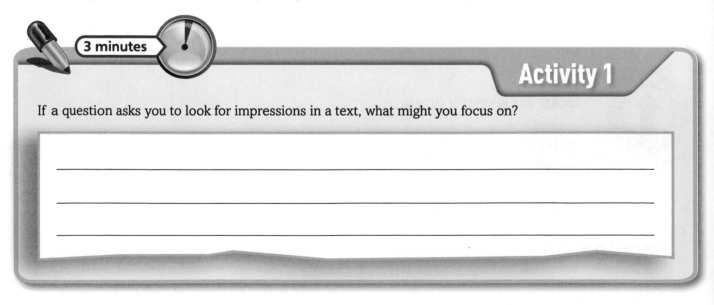

3 minutes

Activity 1

If a question asks you to look for impressions in a text, what might you focus on?

_____

_____

_____

2 minutes

Activity 2

The table below contains a jumbled list of important steps that you will need to follow to help you answer impressions questions. Number them in the correct order.

Write your answer, making sure you track the text chronologically.	
Read the question, highlighting the key words.	
If it will help you, annotate the highlighted sections in the passage to clarify your impressions.	
Read the passage, highlighting the areas where you are given an impression.	

If you are looking at language and words, it is important to quote a short word or phrase and then make it clear what impression the word or phrase creates. Remember never to use long quotations in your answer.

If you are given a text with a picture, you might want to consider what impressions the picture creates.

Remember: continually use the key word 'impressions' from the question to make sure the examiner knows you are on task.

15 minutes

Activity 3

The picture below was taken following a holiday to Skegness.

What you think

Focus on the people

Only write about the picture

What impression do you get of the people in the picture?

Write your impressions in the table below: the first one has been done for you.

Section of the picture	Impression given
The man with the glasses is grimacing	Not everyone is satisfied with the holiday
The woman in the white T-shirt who is flushed and smiling	
The woman in the lilac coat who is pointing	
The man in the striped jumper looks like he is daydreaming	
Many people have grey hair	
The younger lady in the blue jumper	
People looking happy and healthy	

15 minutes

Activity 4

Read the advertisement opposite about Alnwick Castle.

1   Track through the text methodically. Highlight any words or phrases that give you an impression of the place.

2   Record your impressions and evidence in the table below.

Impression	Evidence/Reason

3 Now consider the following exam question.

What impression do you get of Alnwick Castle? *(10 marks)*

4 Using the table you have already completed, write up your answer to the exam question, referring to the grade criteria on page vii as you write.

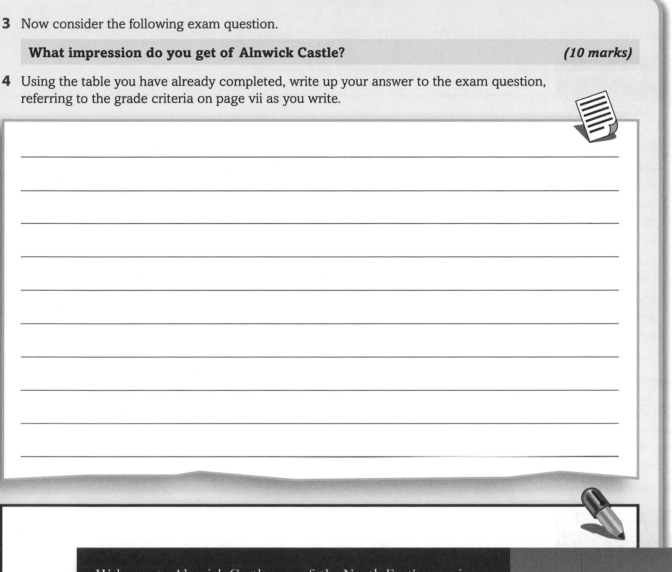

Welcome to Alnwick Castle, one of the North East's premier tourist attractions with around 200,000 visitors each year. It is the centre of a modern and thriving business but remains at the heart of the local community. To many people, on their first sight of this glorious medieval castle, it can seem foreboding, and certainly its history lacks nothing in drama and intrigue. Some of you may recognise us as a film location, for everything from Harry Potter to Elizabeth to Becket to Blackadder.

Bought by the Percy family in 1309, it has played an important role in local history throughout the ages. Today, Alnwick Castle is very much a living castle, at the heart of thriving estates and businesses and it is still our family home, as it has been for seven hundred years, an anniversary which we proudly celebrate this year.

There is much to see and do – history, fine art, fantastic scenery, fun for the children, a wide choice of refreshment options, shopping and exploring. I hope this article gives you a taste of our much-loved castle, it is home to the Duke and Duchess of Northumberland and their family and as the second largest inhabited castle in the country, is often referred to as 'the Windsor of the North'. We hope you can join us for an unforgettable day out soon.

http://www.alnwickcastle.com

GradeStudio

Read these two student answers to the exam question you answered in Activity 4.

A* grade answer

Student 1

We immediately get the impression that Alnwick Castle is a first class tourist destination as they claim it is a 'premier tourist attraction'. The text informs us that the castle receives '200,000 visitors each year' which gives the impression of popularity and success. Despite being particularly old 'seven hundred years…medieval' it has been carefully preserved and is central to the local community 'the centre of a modern and thriving business'. The appearance of the castle gives an impressive but also imposing impression on the reader as it is described as 'glorious' and 'foreboding '. Clearly a success in the world of film and TV, this notion of success and glamour is conveyed as the castle has been used in a number of films from 'Harry Potter to Elizabeth to Becket'. We get the impression that the castle caters for all interests, mentioning 'history, fine art, fantastic scenery, fun for the children, a wide choice of refreshment'. Finally we get the impression that the castle and the experience it brings will be memorable and 'unforgettable'.

Examiner comment 1

The student tracks through the text chronologically and includes a wide range of different impressions. The ideas are all well supported and the student successfully manages to stack more than one different impression within one sentence. The student continually refers to the question and ensures that every point is well supported with relevant ideas and details. This answer is well handled, perceptive and purposeful and is awarded A*.

C grade answer

Student 2

We get the impression that this is a great castle and that it's really old. We also get the impression that it's fairly popular as it has 200,000 visitors each year. There are lots of things to do for the whole family from shopping to exploring so we get the impression that it is trying to attract lots of people. The castle seems alive as it is described as having 'heart'. The castle has been popular with TV directors as it has been used in programmes like Blackadder.

Examiner comment 2

The student refers to the question on a number of occasions and is always focused on the question. The student selects a number of key words and ideas that create impressions, and embeds these into their answer. The impressions created are correct and supported. This student needs to develop the level of detail in their answer to move up the grades.

1 Compare the answers from Students 1 and 2. What are the key differences between the C and A* answer?

Activity 5

Look at the answer you completed on Alnwick Castle in Activity 4, and the grade criteria on page vii. Read through your answer and think about how it meets the criteria. This should help you focus on the things that will help you improve the way you structure your answers. Write down three ways you could improve your answer in the future.

Think about the features identified in the examiner comments and compare them to your own answer. Highlight any comments that you feel you have achieved.

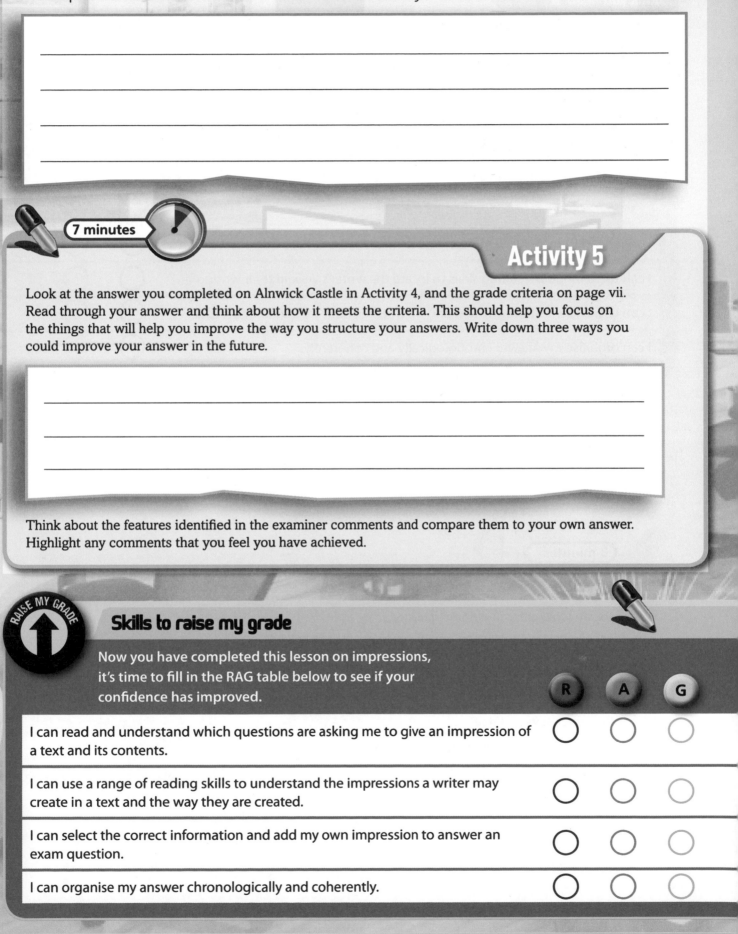

Skills to raise my grade

Now you have completed this lesson on impressions, it's time to fill in the RAG table below to see if your confidence has improved.

	R	A	G
I can read and understand which questions are asking me to give an impression of a text and its contents.	○	○	○
I can use a range of reading skills to understand the impressions a writer may create in a text and the way they are created.	○	○	○
I can select the correct information and add my own impression to answer an exam question.	○	○	○
I can organise my answer chronologically and coherently.	○	○	○

3 Viewpoint and attitude

Skills to raise my grade

RAISE MY GRADE ↑

Fill in the RAG table below to show how confident you are in the following areas:	R	A	G
I understand which questions want me to focus on the writer's viewpoint or attitude.	◯	◯	◯
I can use a range of reading skills to locate the writer's view in their writing.	◯	◯	◯
I can use evidence from the text and then write about their view or attitude.	◯	◯	◯
I can organise my answer chronologically and coherently.	◯	◯	◯

Before you answer questions on viewpoint and attitude, you need to understand what message the writer is trying to get across to their readers.

In this lesson you will practise focusing on a writer's viewpoint or their attitude towards a specific subject, person or place. You will then develop your skills for attitude and viewpoint questions so you are able to identify how to improve your grade.

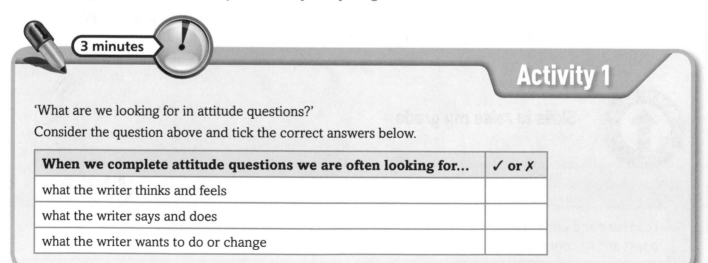

3 minutes

Activity 1

'What are we looking for in attitude questions?'
Consider the question above and tick the correct answers below.

When we complete attitude questions we are often looking for...	✓ or ✗
what the writer thinks and feels	
what the writer says and does	
what the writer wants to do or change	

Activity 2

3 minutes

In order to understand the viewpoints and attitudes of a writer, you have to try to imagine the thoughts and feelings they may have been experiencing at the time.

Match the words and phrases to the most appropriate thoughts and feelings by drawing lines between the two.

Words and phrases	Thoughts and feelings
The whole experience was a nightmare.	Overwhelmed, exhilarated, buzzing
I had a great time on holiday.	Dreadful, dire, horrid
Moving was stressful but the new house was great.	Confused, bewildered, unsure
I had absolutely no idea what to do next.	Happy, cheerful, joyful
I was so pleased to see my friends.	Powerless, helpless, unfair
After the ride I had such an adrenalin rush.	Difficult at first, then rewarding
It was so unfair. She did not deserve to win.	Relaxed, rejuvenated, content

Activity 3

15 minutes

Read the article below called 'A Day at the Zoo' and the exam question that follows it.

A Day at the Zoo by Nicola Holaday

I have to be honest, when a close friend of mine mentioned that we were going to Blackpool Zoo for the day, I was not too impressed. I had visited a number of zoos as a small child and could only remember the overpowering smell of animal dung ... But Blackpool Zoo changed all of my misconceptions. We had a brilliant day and thoroughly enjoyed visiting the array of creatures which all seemed to be well cared for and healthy. The animal enclosures were spacious, the staff were all knowledgeable and we will certainly be visiting again.

What are the writer's thoughts and feelings about Blackpool Zoo? *(5 marks)**

*These exam questions would normally be marked out of 10, but to help you perfect your technique, we are only concentrating on what to include in your answer and how to set it out.

Look at the student answers below and match the examiner comments to the appropriate answers.

Student 1

The writer initially feels concerned about the day at the zoo because they suggest they are not 'impressed'. The writer remembers the smell of zoos 'dung' they visited as a child and feels a little nauseous. The writer feels that Blackpool has successfully changed their views 'changed all of my misconceptions' and it is clear they now feel differently. Finally the writer admits to having a 'brilliant day' because the animals are 'healthy' and this suggests that they feel the experience of the zoo has been most enjoyable.

Student 2

The writer feels worried about the visit to the zoo. They also feel worried about the smell at the zoo. They soon feel that the zoo is great and they think that the animals are well looked after.

Examiner comment A

This student continually mentions the words 'feels' to convince us that they are on task, but does not include any information to support the feelings and rarely develops their ideas. The answer is very short and although the student is on task, they need to include much more detail and information.

Examiner comment B

The student tracks through the text picking up a range of different quotations and these are clearly included in their answer. The student helpfully refers to the writer throughout their answer and this helps us get the impression that they are on task. Continually mentioning the words 'feels' also convinces us that the student is on task and that they are consciously including a range of different feelings to support their quotes. The student covers a range of different feelings in their answer.

1   Which examiner comment matches each of the student answers?

Student 1	Examiner comment:
Student 2	Examiner comment:

2   Based on all the sample student answers and the examiner comments you have read in this lesson, write down three useful tips that will help you answer this type of question in the future.

Viewpoint and attitude – my top tips

- _____
- _____
- _____

20 minutes

Activity 4

Now you have analysed a number of sample student answers, you need to work through an activity which will help you build your skills towards completing an answer of your own.

You are going to read the review *Driven to Distraction* and answer the following exam question. The key words of the question have been underlined for you.

What are Liz Hunt's thoughts and feelings about Jeremy Clarkson? *(10 marks)*

Liz Hunt thinks Jeremy Clarkson is similar to her

BOOKS > reviews

Driven to Distraction by Jeremy Clarkson
By Liz Hunt 09 Oct 2009

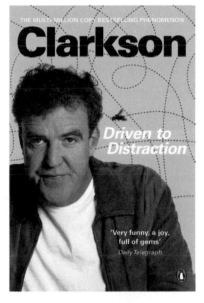

A scart lead brought us together. It was his insight into this infuriating piece of technology that confirmed a meeting of minds – and the moment that my hatred of Jeremy Clarkson vanished. Suddenly, I found myself able to overlook the wire-wool hair, that chin and those jeans. Yes! Someone understands, I thought, and how strange that it should be Clarkson whom I thought only ever wrote about cars. He does write about cars, of course. *Driven to Distraction* is a collection of his motoring columns for *The Sunday Times*, and I was distracted by the cars – the BM this and XKR that. Distracted and bored. Because, as Clarkson acknowledges, 'Women who aren't interested in cars won't read about them'.

When I began my review of his latest book I was initially worried, but I quickly realised that he is very funny and his well-honed political incorrectness a joy. He has also perfected the knack of expressing some fundamental truths about life that provide priceless 'Eureka' moments for the reader.

His struggle to master his photographic printer, traipsing back and forth to PC World to buy ever more expensive and sophisticated software to produce ever more useless pictures, will ring true with anyone who longs for the days when you dropped off the film at Boots and picked up your snaps a day later.

He has his softer moments – yes, really. Who would have guessed that his favourite film was that soppy – *Local Hero*? Or that he has a romantic passion for space that goes beyond hi-tech gizmos. And I was hugely entertained by his childlike pleasure in driving a JCB, working the levers and the dials furiously while running out of things to dig up.

What began as an assignment from hell developed into an enjoyable journey. *Driven to Distraction* is the perfect bathroom book, to dip in and out of, as and when, and discover your own Eureka moments with a man, whom I suspect, is not so far off becoming a national treasure.

1 Highlight or underline words and phrases in the article that you think suggest what the writer, Liz Hunt, thinks and feels about Jeremy Clarkson.

2 Note down in the table what you think these words and phrases suggest about her feelings. The first example has been done for you.

Words and phrases	What this suggests about her feelings
'meeting of minds'	Liz Hunt thinks Jeremy Clarkson is similar to her

3 Now write up your answer to the exam question, making sure you clearly state the writer's thoughts and feelings, giving evidence to support what you are suggesting.

_____

_____

_____

_____

_____

_____

_____

_____

_____

_____

_____

_____

_____

7 minutes

Activity 5

You will now be given the opportunity to review and assess your work.

1 First, check your answer from Activity 4 against this success criteria table for viewpoint and attitude questions.

	✓ or ✗
Did you clearly start your answer by mentioning the name of the writer and Jeremy Clarkson?	
Did you track through the text in order?	
Did you come up with a range of **different** thoughts and feelings?	
Did you notice the change in attitude from the writer's initial view?	
Did you support each thought and feeling with a quote or evidence from the text?	
Did you make at least 5–6 points?	
How much of the text did you cover?	

2 Now, in your own answer, highlight the evidence that you have included and tick the thought or feeling that goes with the evidence. Each time you have a tick there should be a highlighted word or phrase to support your idea.

3 Have you included any of the following words in your answer to describe Liz Hunt's thoughts and feelings about Jeremy Clarkson? Write down a brief definition of what each of these words means.

Word	Definition
Admiration	
Appreciation	
Inspiring	
Respect	
Entertaining	

4 Once you have assessed your own work, write down one or two tips that will help you improve next time.

- _____

- _____

Read this film review for *The Spy Next Door* and the exam question below.

What are the writer's thoughts and feelings about Jackie Chan's film *The Spy Next Door*?

(10 marks)

Film Review: The Spy Next Door

The Spy Next Door should be released straight onto DVD to save Chan any further embarrassment because the message from this massive flop is clear: his career is over.

It's sad to see such a likeable star wasting their talent, especially one as pleasant as Chan, but that sadness quickly turns to desperation during *The Spy Next Door*. It is replaced by frustration, and then annoyance as you realise this film is not going to get any better.

Chan plays Bob Ho, a Chinese spy who has been working for the CIA and is now retiring so he can settle down with his girlfriend, Gillian, who lives next door and doesn't know he's a spy. She thinks he's a pen importer. Around her, Bob acts like a boring geek, wears glasses, and hides his super-spy abilities. Gillian loves the fact that he's normal and dependable, not like her ex-husband, who ran off and left her with three kids.

Gillian has to go out of town because her father's in hospital and Bob volunteers to babysit. You can pretty much guess what happens next…

A Russian terrorist escapes CIA custody and is looking for a top-secret code that Gillian's son accidentally downloaded from Bob's computer. To cut a long story mercifully short, Bob must save the children – and the world!

Chan is fun to watch when he's fighting; every now and then in *The Spy Next Door* you catch a glimpse of why you usually like his movies. Then the glimpse disappears and it's back to the domestic troubles, which are routine, unimaginative and depressing. A big thumbs down all round.

Lesley Dodds
A very lucky: ☆☆☆☆☆

Read the student answer below which has been awarded a grade C.

C grade answer

Lesley Dodds thinks that the film is a 'massive flop' and that by the end of the film she felt filled with 'desperation'. She also felt that the film was pretty predictable 'You can pretty much guess what happens next...' She think that Jackie Chan's films are usually good as people 'usually like his movies' but that this one gets 'A big thumbs down all round.'

What would you add to the answer to improve it to an A*? Refer to the grade descriptions on page vii to help you make your changes.

_____

_____

_____

_____

_____

_____

_____

_____

_____

RAISE MY GRADE

Skills to raise my grade

Now you have completed this lesson on viewpoint and attitude, it's time to fill in the RAG table below to see if your confidence has improved.

	R	A	G
I understand which questions want me to focus on the writer's viewpoint or attitude.	○	○	○
I can use a range of reading skills to locate the writer's view in their writing.	○	○	○
I can use evidence from the text and then write about their view or attitude.	○	○	○
I can organise my answer chronologically and coherently.	○	○	○

4 Intended audience

Skills you need ▶

You must show that you can:
- explore the range of potential audiences who might read or use a text
- understand who a text is aimed at
- organise an answer for this type of question

RAISE MY GRADE ↑

Skills to raise my grade

Fill in the RAG table below to show how confident you are in the following areas:	R	A	G
I understand which questions want me to focus on working out who the audience is.	○	○	○
I can use a range of reading skills that help me locate different areas of a text that might appeal to different people.	○	○	○
I can use the evidence from the text and any pictures to support my ideas about the audience.	○	○	○
I can organise my answer chronologically and coherently.	○	○	○

Before you try to answer questions on intended audience, you need to understand the range of different readers who might use a text.

In this lesson you will practise focusing on understanding the range of different people that the writer might be targeting. You will then learn how to structure answers for this type of question before focusing on how to improve your grade.

3 minutes

Activity 1

Write down a definition of the word 'audience'.

_____

_____

If you are trying to work out the audience of a text, make sure you cover a range of different people. You might focus include some of the following:

▶ teenagers
▶ students
▶ pensioners
▶ a specific gender group
▶ people with a specific interest, e.g. cyclists
▶ people of a specific age group.

20 minutes

When we start to answer questions about the 'intended audience' it is often useful to ask yourself **who** the text is aimed at.

Read the following advertisement for a 5-star luxury family holiday complex *The Sage* and the exam question that follows it.

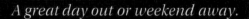

The Sage

A great day out or weekend away.

At *The Sage* we have it all. Take a leisurely stroll with your partner around our award-winning, adult-only gardens or spend a relaxing afternoon enjoying tea and cakes in our famous *Teaspot*. Run wild in the fairy woodlands or treat your feet to our hot rock barefoot walk. If you like to get an adrenalin kick, try out our water sports – you can feel the thrill of a speed boat or even take a computerised pedalo across the lake to the magical island theme park. Children (with their adventurous parents) can spend hours in our corn maze or adventure playground, while shopaholics can enjoy some indulgent retail therapy in our numerous designer outlets.

If you want some peace, leave the children at home and enjoy a relaxing day in our state-of-the-art spa. You're sure to come out looking and feeling ten years younger!

If you don't want the luxury to end you can even stay overnight in our magnificent 5* hotel, where the top floor's computerised games room and casino can be enjoyed by all.

The Sage – we've got it all.

The Sage – we've got it all.

Who is *The Sage* advertisement aimed at? Support your ideas with evidence from the text. *(10 marks)*

1 Before you begin trying to answer this exam question, think about the following prompt questions.

  a The title uses the phrase 'A great day out or weekend away'. Who are they appealing to?

  b 'leisurely stroll': what type of people might stroll?

  c 'adult-only gardens': who might this feature appeal to?

  d 'spend a relaxing afternoon enjoying tea and cakes': what types of people would enjoy this?

  e 'Run wild in the fairy woodlands': what type of person runs wild?

  f 'get an adrenalin kick': what type of person is looking for this activity?

  g 'magical island theme park': who specifically does this appeal to?

  h 'retail therapy in the designer outlets': who would enjoy this?

  i 'leave the children at home … enjoy … state of the art spa': who would enjoy this?

  j 'computerised games room and casino': what type of person would enjoy this?

  k Are there any other words and phrases mentioned in the text that might appeal to a different type of person/groups?

1 Now complete this table with possible audiences for the advert and evidence to support your ideas.

Who is the text aimed at?	Evidence to support your idea

2 Write down **three** useful tips that will help you answer this type of question in the future.

Intended audience – My top tips

- _____
- _____
- _____

20 minutes

Activity 3

1 Look at the exam question below and spend 1 minute annotating it to show that you understand what it is asking you to do.

Who is the advert trying to attract to experience *Go Ape*? *(10 marks)*

Now read the article about *Go Ape* on page 27.

The article immediately seeks to attract people who are daring or adventurous.

GO APE

What is Go Ape?

It's not in the dictionary, but if it was, *Go Ape* would be described as a 'high-wire forest adventure'.

We build giant obstacle courses up in the trees using ladders, walkways, bridges and tunnels made of wood, rope and super-strong wire, and top it all off with the country's best zip lines (including the longest at 426 metres – check it out on YouTube).

We then kit people out with harnesses, pulleys and karabiners, give them a 30-minute safety briefing and training and let them loose into the forest canopy, free to swing through the trees. Of course, instructors are always on hand, regularly patrolling the forests (not in monkey suits unfortunately!).

The result is spectacular. The *Go Ape* experience gets the adrenalin pumping, gets people out of their comfort zones and above all, it's just great fun.

Can you Go Ape?

Participant restrictions

Minimum age – 10yrs
Minimum height – 1.4m (4ft7")
Maximum weight – 20.5 stones (130kg)
The maximum number of participants per session is 14. Don't worry if you are going with more people; you can simply book more sessions to cater for the number of people you are going with.

At *Go Ape* we use harnesses to make sure you're nice and safe throughout your time on the course. The maximum waist measurement of the harness is 110cm and the leg loops (which go around the top of your thighs) is 70cm.

Supervision ratios

Under 18-yr-olds must be supervised by a participating adult.

One participating adult can supervise EITHER two under 18 year olds (where one or both children are 10–15 years old) OR up to five 16–17-year-olds. Participating adults may not supervise from the ground.

Fitness

Doing *Go Ape* does require a degree of physical fitness, but if you can climb up a rope ladder you should be fine.

1 Highlight or underline words and phrases in the advert that you think suggest the different people that the article is trying to attract.

2 Note down the different people or groups these words or phrases are trying to attract in the table below. The first example has been done for you.

Words and phrases	Target audience groups
'high-wire forest adventure'	The article immediately seeks to attract people who are daring or adventurous

3 Now write up your answer to the exam question, making sure you give evidence to support what you are suggesting.

Activity 4

You will now be given the opportunity to review and assess your work.

1 First, check your answer against this success criteria table for intended audience questions.

	✓ or ✗
Did you include a range of potential audiences?	
Did you work through the whole text chronologically?	
Did you include evidence from the text to support your ideas?	
Did you find any words or phrases that might appeal to certain people?	

2 Now annotate your work by highlighting the evidence that you have included and ticking the identified audience that goes with the evidence. Each time you have a tick there should be a highlighted word or phrase to support your idea

3 Look at the grade criteria on page vii. List the features that you have included in your work.

_____

_____

_____

_____

_____

4 Which grade is your answer closest to? Explain why.

_____

_____

_____

_____

_____

5 Once you have assessed your work, write down one or two tips that will help you improve next time.

- _____

- _____

Look back at the advertisement for *The Sage* on page 25. The exam question for this text was:

> **Who is *The Sage* advertisement aimed at? Support your ideas with evidence from the text.**
>
> *(10 marks)*

Below is a typical C grade student answer for this exam question.

C grade answer

> The text is written for and aimed at people who are interested in going away and having time out for themselves. The text is also aimed at people who like gardens as there are some there. The text is aimed at people who like to pamper themselves as there are lots of pampering things to do there. It is also aimed at people who like sport and excitement as there are some pretty cool things like computerised pedalos. The text is written for people who like to gamble as there is a Casino.

1 Having read the answer, what do you think is missing? How do you think the candidate could increase their grade? Look back at the mark scheme on page vii.

2 Look again at the grade C student answer. Now look at the examiner comments below that match it and discuss these in a group. Think about what you could do to improve the answer that will take in everything the examiner has noted.

C grade answer

Look at the entire answer. In almost every sentence, there is a clear audience identified, but the candidate does not link their audience to the text by giving evidence

Clear audience group identified, but the candidate does not link their idea to the text

The text is written for and aimed at people who are interested in going away and having time out for themselves. The text is also aimed at people who like gardens as there are some there. The text is aimed at people who like to pamper themselves as there are lots of pampering things to do there. It is also aimed at people who like sport and excitement as there are some pretty cool things like computerised pedalos. The text is written for people who like to gamble as there is a Casino.

The candidate does successfully refer to the question

There is some attempt to give evidence here

3 Write your improved answer in the space below.

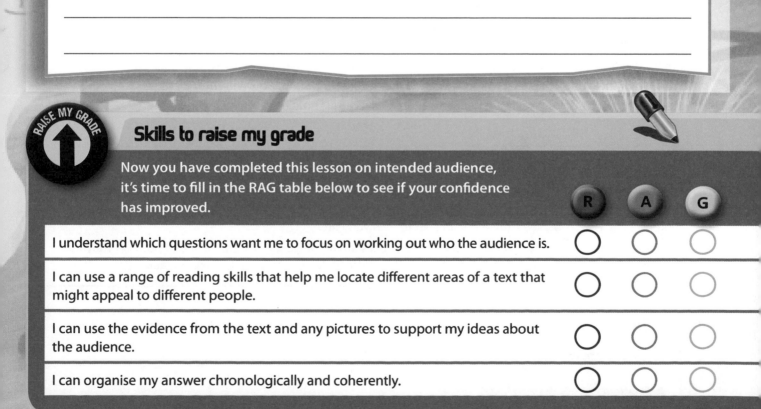

Skills to raise my grade

Now you have completed this lesson on intended audience, it's time to fill in the RAG table below to see if your confidence has improved.

	R	A	G
I understand which questions want me to focus on working out who the audience is.	○	○	○
I can use a range of reading skills that help me locate different areas of a text that might appeal to different people.	○	○	○
I can use the evidence from the text and any pictures to support my ideas about the audience.	○	○	○
I can organise my answer chronologically and coherently.	○	○	○

5 Analysis of persuasive techniques

Skills to raise my grade

Fill in the RAG table below to show how confident you are in the following areas:	R	A	G
I understand which questions want me to focus on *how* a writer persuades a reader.	○	○	○
I can detect a range of persuasive techniques within a text.	○	○	○
I can work out how a writer's techniques work.	○	○	○
I can use the evidence from the text to support my ideas when focusing on persuasive techniques.	○	○	○
I know how to organise my answer, making sure I write chronologically and coherently.	○	○	○

Before you tackle any questions where you have to analyse the writer's techniques, it is essential that you are familiar with a range of persuasive devices. In these questions you need to understand the message the writer is trying to get across to their readers, but more importantly *how* they get that message across.

In this lesson you will revise persuasive techniques, practise focusing on the writer's skills and the ways they might appeal to, persuade or manipulate a reader. You will then develop your skills for persuasion questions so you are able to identify how to improve your grade.

10 minutes

Activity 1

Think about where we see or use persuasion in everyday life.

1 Here are just a few suggestions of the types of persuasive things that we might see in our everyday lives. For each item, write down the type of appeal they will make and how each will persuade.

- Advert _____

- Charity appeal _____

- Leaflets _____

- Brochures _____

- Flyers _____

- Letters _____

3 minutes

Activity 2

1 Read the persuasive features listed in the table below. Match them to the actions which each feature creates in a persuasive text.

Feature		Actions
Structure		You have to work out the writer's views and how they try to influence the reader to feel the same.
Headline/title		Look out for facts, opinions, examples, statistics and think about how they make you feel – this is the actual information included.
Content		Think about the order of the information – is it helpful and how?
Tone		Find key words and phrases used by the writer and think about the effect they have.
Pictures		Look at the way something is written – the tone might be abusive, sarcastic, calm, emotional, sad, etc.
Presentation		Has the writer used any of the following: puns, questions, direct appeal (you/we). It is only persuasive if the words/phrases are effective.
The writer's approach to the topic		These can add visual support to a text. You have to look at them closely and be very specific here, for example '*The --- of … persuades me because …*'
Language		Look at the overall way in which the information is set out – ask yourself whether the appearance of the article persuades you – if so, how does it look professional? Does it use logos?

You might be given bullet points with your exam question so you have to focus specifically on one of the features above. Alternatively, if you are asked to complete a general persuasion/'How does the writer…' question, the list above gives you an excellent range of things to cover.

10 minutes

1 Look at this advertisement for Chris Hoy's new book below. Identify the persuasive
   features and explain **why** they might persuade you to buy the book.

Olympic Champion Chris Hoy's Autobiography

RRP £18.99

Review

Praise for Chris Hoy:

'It's hard to think of a more deserving recipient of success than Chris Hoy' *The Guardian*

'Who is my sporting hero?' It's Chris Hoy.' He's an inspiration...a real role model' *Team-mate Victoria Pendleton*

'To appreciate Hoy, you need to understand his exercise of self-control, plus those nagging doubts, for it is this potent combination that has driven him to such heights' *The Times*

Product Description

As the first Briton to win three Olympic golds at the same Games since 1908, Scotland's Chris Hoy has become a beacon for British sporting achievement. His autobiography charts his life from 7-year-old BMX fanatic, supported by a devoted dad and local cycling club, through paralysing self-doubt and a major career overhaul, to the sport's holy grail. Chris Hoy is a genuine sporting superhero – and he's British.

In his autobiography, Hoy returns to his roots as a child fully engaged with the BMX craze of the Eighties; when, even as a seven-year-old, his will to succeed allied to an unyielding mental strength set him apart from other youngsters of his age. A promising rower and rugby player in school, it was when he joined his first local cycling club and spent most weekends of the year competing in national events from Blackpool to Bristol that the seeds of his future career were sown. With the devoted support of his family, Hoy drove himself to the pinnacle of his sport at the same time as British track cycling established itself as a pioneering force on the world stage. In the lead up to London 2012, there is no sporting icon better placed to demonstrate what it takes to reach the top than Chris Hoy.

10 minutes

Read the article '4 simple steps to super skin' below.

4 simple steps to super skin

Follow these 4 simple steps to improve your skin!

Protect your skin. Always use sunscreen. Sunscreen protects your skin from the sun, and reduces your chance of skin cancer, but did you also know that this reduces the chance of signs of early ageing? 90% of premature ageing is caused by the sun. Sure, it may not be something that you're thinking of when you're in your teens, but you'll be glad you did in 15 years.

Stop the soap. Find a facial cleanser that's best for your skin type, and we mean you too, boys! Many teens find that oily skin is their main concern, if this is your problem look for a gel-based cleanser. Make sure you wash your face in the morning and at night. Girls – never sleep in your makeup: you'll regret it in the morning.

Moisturise your face. Always moisturise after you wash and dry your face. If your skin is very oily, you may choose to just moisturise in the morning.

Use a weekly mask and exfoliate. A mask deep cleans your pores, while an exfoliator removes the top layer of skin. Make sure you are gentle; if you over scrub, your skin may break out even further. Use only once a week for perfect skin.

Vicky Miller – Dermatologist

How does the article encourage teenagers and young people to look after their skin? The persuasive features have been listed for you in the table below. Think about how each of the selected features encourages young people and teenagers to look after their skin and write your explanations into the table.

Persuasive feature/words/phrases	How it persuades
4 simple steps to super skin	
Protect your skin	
Sunscreen protects your skin … reduces your chance of skin cancer … reduces the chance of signs of early ageing	
90% of premature ageing is caused by the sun	
we mean you too, boys!	
Girls – never sleep in your makeup	
Always moisturise after you wash and dry your face	
A mask deep cleans your pores, while an exfoliator removes the top layer of skin	

Activity 5

Read the exam question below and jot down what you think it is asking you to do.

> **Read the advert 'Save yourself more than just a packet'.**
> **How does it persuade you to stop smoking?**
> **You should think about the following in your answer:**
> • **what the advert says**
> • **how the advert is presented.** *(10 marks)*

Read the advert 'Save yourself more than just a packet...' below.

Save yourself more than just a packet...

Next time you light up, feel your pulse within a minute: it will be quicker. Your heart has to work harder and the likelihood of a blood clot increases with each cigarette, as does the amount of carbon monoxide in your body. All of these are risk factors for heart disease, but once you're hooked it's so hard to stop.

The younger you start smoking, the more damage there will be to your body when you get older. Here are seven reasons to quit.

1 You'll be healthier and less out of breath because smoking decreases your lung capacity.

2 You'll save yourself a packet. Smoking 20 a day for a year costs around £2,190.

3 You'll look better. Chemicals in cigarettes restrict blood flow to your skin. Smokers have more wrinkled and saggy faces by the time they're in their mid-20s.

4 Quitting helps save the planet. Deforestation due to tobacco production accounts for nearly 5% of overall deforestation in the developing world, according to research published in medical journal *The BMJ*.

5 Someone who starts smoking at 15 is three times more likely to die from cancer than someone who starts smoking in their mid-20s.

6 The younger you start smoking, the more damage there will be to your body as an adult.

7 Not smoking will make you instantly more attractive. Most people prefer kissing non-smokers.

Stop today – save a life – your life.

Now answer the exam question above.

_____

_____

_____

_____

_____

_____

_____

_____

_____

_____

_____

10 minutes

Activity 6

1 Read the student answer, then use the following questions to think about and annotate the answer.

- Did the writer track through the text in order?
- Did the writer use the key word 'persuade' throughout their answer?
- Did the writer come up with a range of **different** pieces of evidence?
- Did the writer explain how **each** of these pieces of evidence can persuade?
- Did the writer make at least 5–6 points?

Student 1

The article persuades you to stop smoking in a wide number of different ways. The article says that there are lots of dangers to your health and they give a list of the things that could happen like 'carbon monoxide'. Another way that we are persuaded is that the article says that 'you'll be healthier' so this persuades people to stop because no one wants to be unhealthy as you might die younger and you might suffer one of the horrible things it mentions in the article. The article uses lots of facts like 'Smoking 20 a day for a year costs £2,190.' and this persuades us to stop smoking because we'll have more money to spend on better stuff. The article is presented in a way that it will help you stop smoking because there are lots of good things to help us read like bullet points. The sentences are short so we read on and the paragraphs are short too.

◻ grade

2 Now look at the grade criteria table on page vii. What grade would you award this student answer? Write it in the box above.

Look back at the advert for Chris Hoy's book in Activity 3 (page 34). A possible exam question for a text like this could be:

> **How does the advert for Chris Hoy's book persuade us to buy it?** *(10 marks)*

1 Read these sample student answers to this exam question. Match each student answer with the correct examiner comments that follow. There is an extra comment which does not belong to either answer.

Student 1

The advert persuades us to buy the book because he is a well-known cyclists so we think that his book will be fairly decent. The union jack on his outfit makes us think that this cyclist was made in our country so people might like that and it might make them want to buy the book. Chris Hoy has a number of famous sponsors like Adidas so if they are happy to support him then he must be decent and this helps to persuade us to buy it. It tells us that he is a role model so this persuades us that he must have an interesting book. Lots of other groups like The Times and The Guardian have reviewed it and liked it so this is persuasive too. We learn he is Olympic Champion and if he is the best we might want to learn how he did it which is also persuasive.

Student 2

When we look at the front cover of Hoy's book we see a number of visual techniques that may persuade any reader to purchase this book. He is Olympic Champion suggesting he is top of his game and the best in the world, such a title will persuade people, that his book must be of interest to any sport's fan. His suit is made from the union jack which appeal to our national pride and persuades readers to buy the book and support one of our sporting heroes. The statement at the bottom "How I lived the dream…" is also a subtle persuasive technique, we subliminally wonder if we will be given some of the secrets of his success which appeals to our inquisitive nature. Hoy's stance and the angle of the picture creates an image of Hoy as being almost superhuman and the height of physical success, persuading people who hope to mirror his achievements to buy his book. He looks confident and his confidence in the book is highly persuasive too.
The Review and Product description are also highly persuasive. Highly renowned reviewers like the Times have included a great deal of praise about the book and the person 'It's hard to think of a more deserving recipient of success than Chris Hoy'. He is recognised as a "hero" and an "inspiration" which is real praise and would encourage anyone unfamiliar with chris Hoy to support one of Britain's "role model". He is also described as a "beacon for British sporting achievement. The text also cleverley lnks to the upcoming Olympic Games (set in London) and this is a final persuasive technique for sporting fans as we will learn "what it takes to reach the top."

Examiner comment 1

This answer is too short. It lacks detail and explanation in places and there is limited focus on the question, despite some references to the text. Grade D

Examiner comment 2

There are some clear observations about the text and some of these are usually linked to the question. The candidate does not always explore how the features they have spotted will persuade us and sometimes their ideas are not clearly expressed. Grade C

Examiner comment 3

This answer has been well thought out and is packed with sensible suggestions as to how the poster persuades people to purchase the cereal. Each sentence is carefully linked to an aspect of the text and is not only supported with sensible explanations but is well rooted in the question. Grade A.

1 Look again at the answers. Highlight or underline each time you see any link to the question or a mention of persuade.

2 Now, using a different colour, highlight or underline the links the students have made to the poster. Look carefully at the answers: the highlighted words and phrases should indicate the balance of links and explanations needed in your own answers.

RAISE MY GRADE

Skills to raise my grade

Now you have completed this lesson on analysing persuasive techniques, it's time to fill in the RAG table below to see if your confidence has improved.

	R	A	G
I understand which questions want me to focus on *how* a writer persuades a reader.	◯	◯	◯
I can detect a range of persuasive techniques within a text.	◯	◯	◯
I can work out how a writer's techniques work.	◯	◯	◯
I can use the evidence from the text to support my ideas when focusing on persuasive techniques.	◯	◯	◯
I know how to organise my answer, making sure I write chronologically and coherently.	◯	◯	◯

6 Comparison and evaluation of texts

Skills to raise my grade

RAISE MY GRADE

Fill in the RAG table below to show how confident you are in the following areas:

	R	A	G
I understand which questions want me to focus on two different texts.	○	○	○
I can understand what these questions are asking me to do.	○	○	○
I can confidently handle two texts and know how to use the material to answer questions.	○	○	○
I can use the evidence from the texts to support my ideas when comparing/evaluating texts.	○	○	○
I know how to organise my answer, making sure I write chronologically, coherently and use both texts.	○	○	○

Before you tackle any questions where you have to focus on two different texts, it is important that you understand what you need to include in your answer and how to structure your answer. Many candidates struggle with this type of question because they try to include too much information and end up missing the main point of the question.

In these questions you need to understand what the question is asking you to do with the different texts. You may be focusing on comparing the texts, evaluating the information in them, or using the information from both texts to produce a piece of informative or explanatory writing.

In this lesson you will focus on what the questions mean before learning how to structure an answer and what you need to include.

2 minutes

Activity 1

What do the following terms mean? Write down a brief definition of each one.

	Definition
Compare	
Contrast	
Evaluate	

2 minutes

Activity 2

Write down some general features of a text that you could compare. An example is given to start your list:

Tip

In some compare and evaluate questions you will be given a list of bullet points or headings that you are told you could use in your answer. The examiner includes these to help you, so you should use them in your answer. Remember – if you are given a clear instruction, such as how to lay out your answer, you must follow it!

- **use of formal or informal tone** _____
- _____
- _____
- _____

3 minutes

Activity 3

In many compare and evaluate questions you are asked to look for things that are similar or different. Look at the two texts on sleep on page 42. Make a list of similarities and differences in the table below, thinking about the following questions:

- Why has each text been written and who has it been written for?
- What are the differences between the layout and the language?

Similarities	Differences

Symptoms of sleep deprivation

Although a great deal of research has been conducted about sleep and sleeping patterns, there is little evidence to suggest that sleep deprivation can cause physical damage to the body. However, it can affect the way you feel, the way you think and it can also interfere with your school, work and home life.

Feeling tired makes us miserable. It makes us feel lethargic, grumpy, irritable and less able to carry out our normal everyday tasks. Extreme tiredness can make you more vulnerable to depression and anxiety. Your performance at school or work can be drastically affected as your brain struggles to think and work quickly. If you are feeling drowsy, you may be at a greater risk of accidents, for example when driving or using machinery.

You will be less able to complete mental tasks and your ability to reason logically will also deteriorate. Memory is affected by sleep deprivation too. Tasks requiring concentration and effort should still be achievable, but you will find yourself less able to complete simple tasks.

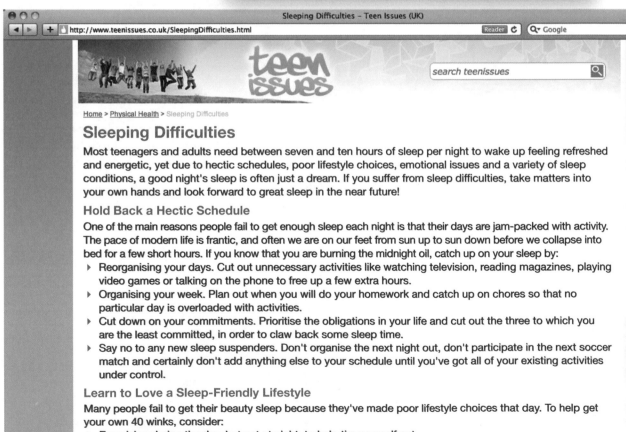

Sleeping Difficulties – Teen Issues (UK)

http://www.teenissues.co.uk/SleepingDifficulties.html

search teenissues

Home > Physical Health > Sleeping Difficulties

Sleeping Difficulties

Most teenagers and adults need between seven and ten hours of sleep per night to wake up feeling refreshed and energetic, yet due to hectic schedules, poor lifestyle choices, emotional issues and a variety of sleep conditions, a good night's sleep is often just a dream. If you suffer from sleep difficulties, take matters into your own hands and look forward to great sleep in the near future!

Hold Back a Hectic Schedule

One of the main reasons people fail to get enough sleep each night is that their days are jam-packed with activity. The pace of modern life is frantic, and often we are on our feet from sun up to sun down before we collapse into bed for a few short hours. If you know that you are burning the midnight oil, catch up on your sleep by:

▸ Reorganising your days. Cut out unnecessary activities like watching television, reading magazines, playing video games or talking on the phone to free up a few extra hours.
▸ Organising your week. Plan out when you will do your homework and catch up on chores so that no particular day is overloaded with activities.
▸ Cut down on your commitments. Prioritise the obligations in your life and cut out the three to which you are the least committed, in order to claw back some sleep time.
▸ Say no to any new sleep suspenders. Don't organise the next night out, don't participate in the next soccer match and certainly don't add anything else to your schedule until you've got all of your existing activities under control.

Learn to Love a Sleep-Friendly Lifestyle

Many people fail to get their beauty sleep because they've made poor lifestyle choices that day. To help get your own 40 winks, consider:

▸ Exercising during the day, but not at night, to help tire yourself out.
▸ Eating enough healthy foods to keep yourself satisfied.
▸ Cutting out caffeinated food and drinks such as tea, coffee or fizzy drinks.
▸ Avoiding "upper" drugs like ecstasy and amphetamines.
▸ Keeping your bedroom temperature cool enough to be comfortable under the duvet.
▸ Getting up at a similar time each morning.
▸ Stopping work at least a half an hour before bedtime.
▸ Sipping non-caffeinated tea before retiring.
▸ Getting a specialised mattress or downy pillow to help you snuggle in.
▸ Taking a lukewarm bath after dinner to help you relax.

Look at the following exam question.

> **These texts have been written to help people who have sleep problems. Compare and contrast them using the following headings:**
> • **What is the purpose of each text?**
> • **Who are the texts written for?**
> • **What are the writers' attitudes towards sleep problems?** *(10 marks)*

Read the sample student answer written in response to this question, and the examiner comments below.

C grade answer

Answer 1

The purpose of the first text is to make people aware of the signs of sleep problems so they are able to see when they are having problems themselves, they might be grumpy or irritable. The purpose of the second text is to make people aware of some of the things they can do if they are having sleep problems themselves, like organising their time better and doing things like not drinking coffee or tea before bed.

The first text is aimed at people who think they might be having sleep problems because they can read the text and then if they have problems they can do something about it. The second text is aimed at people who already know that they have sleep problems as they will be looking for something to do about it.

The writer's attitude towards a lack of sleep in the first text is that it won't damage you but that it will make you feel pretty rubbish. The writer's attitude towards sleep problems in the second text is that if you have a problem then you should do something about it yourself.

Examiner comment 1

This answer is fairly well organised and the student does address each of the bullet points with some detail. There is little textual support (especially for the first two bullets) and the student could benefit from expanding the detail in their answer. They also need to be more specific (see the notes on the second bullet point). Grade C.

1 Write down **three** tips that you think would help the candidate improve their answer.

- _____
- _____
- _____

2 Now look at the next answer, where the student has used the examiner comment to improve their grade. Highlight the points/ideas they have added so you can see how to improve your own answer.

A*   grade answer

Answer 2

What is the purpose of each text?
The purpose of the article is to inform people of the symptoms that people may suffer from if they are having sleep problems. It is factual and makes it clear that the impact of a lack of sleep can have everyday symptoms like being 'grumpy', but that it can also have more severe consequences like being 'more vulnerable to depression'. The purpose of the webpage is to show people that they do not need to suffer unnecessarily from sleep deprivation as there are a wealth of simple solutions to solve any issues. It encourages them to be optimistic and to 'look forward to great sleep in the near future!'

Who are the texts written for?
The article is aimed at anyone who is suffering from the symptoms of sleep deprivation and the information is suitable for people of all ages. The webpage has a broad teenage audience as it was taken from a teenage website (www.teenissues.co.uk). The audience could be teenagers themselves or parents who are worried about their children's sleep.

What are the writers' attitudes towards sleep problems?
The writer's attitude towards sleep problems in the article is that it doesn't have to be a huge burden on your life. It does stress that it can have an impact on things we take for granted, such as 'being less able to carry out our normal everyday tasks'. It also suggests that it doesn't have to always be viewed as something debilitating as 'tasks requiring concentration and effort should still be achievable'. The writer's attitude to sleep problems in the webpage is that individuals need to be proactive when looking for a solution and 'take matters into your own hands'. It also suggests that suffering from sleep difficulties is quite common due to 'hectic schedules' which helps to reasure the reader.

Examiner comment 2

This answer is competently organised and the student has helpfully included headings in their answer as suggested by the task, which helps keep the answer focused and relevant. Each point has been well supported by textual evidence/ supporting detail. The student could have been more concise by making more use of overview in this answer, but it is a thorough and consistent answer which would achieve grade A*.

3 Note down any good pieces of advice that you can use for your own work.

Compare and evaluate – my top tips

- _____
- _____
- _____

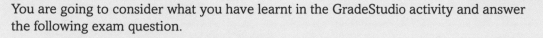

20 minutes

Activity 4

You are going to consider what you have learnt in the GradeStudio activity and answer the following exam question.

These two texts are both reviews of the iPhone. Compare and contrast what the writers think about the iPhone.
Organise your answer into two paragraphs using the following headings.
• **What are the writer's two attitudes towards the iPhone?**
• **What reasons do they give for their attitudes?**   *(10 marks)*

1 Before you start, highlight the key words in the question so you understand how to answer the question and what to include. Then read the two reviews below and on the following page: 'Amy's blog' and 'Apple iPhone 4 Review'.

blog   podcasts   news   comments

Amy's Blog

My Apple iPhone 3 Review

If you are a lover of the iPhone then I suggest you put down this review and walk away as you might find the following rant a little frustrating…

I get so annoyed when people, even experts, get so caught up in iPhone hype. I have been the not-so-proud owner of an iPhone 3 since last November and it is without doubt the biggest load of junk (and waste of money) I have ever owned.

The call quality is dismal, and I mean dismal. Most of my friends have given up phoning me because I can't hear our conversation. The camera quality is even worse, God only knows where the camera has come from but I suggest it has been recycled from something made in the 1980s. Trying to connect to the Internet takes the best part of a day and the battery life is awful. Not only is the life span of the battery poor, but if something goes wrong with the battery you can't take it out to fix it (hey, more money to Apple)!

OK, so it's not all bad, the interface is good, but that's the only positive I can think of and once the novelty of that has worn off, the problems quickly overpower this tiny positive.

So why am I so annoyed? I have to admit, I am a great fan of the mobile phone and when this phone came out I thought it was going to revolutionise the mobile world, so I had to get one. But I have been sorely disappointed. Please people: open your eyes! Unless we moan they'll never improve this piece of junk. Give me a Sony Ericsson, Nokia or Samsung any day, I swear.

Home | News | Sport | Finance | Lifestyle | Culture

News | Reviews | Tech | Advice

Home | Tech | Apple

Apple iPhone 4 Review

Phone rating: ★★★★☆ Excellent

In a nutshell: The iPhone 4 is a flawed beauty. The main improvements are the extra high resolution display, the improved camera, HD video recording, a second camera for video calls and longer battery life. But there are problems getting a signal and it's phenomenally expensive too.

Review: June 2010

Another year, another iPhone. Released on the 24th June 2010 in the UK, the iPhone 4 is in many ways the best iPhone so far. But it's also the most expensive.

There's also a problem with the new design. The stainless steel body of the handset acts as an antenna and Apple claim this will help to improve reception of mobile signals. But only if you hold it the right way, because if you place your hand over the bottom left corner of the phone, you'll see your signal drop to zero. Apple's official statement is not reassuring: 'Avoid gripping it in the lower left corner in a way that covers both sides of the black strip in the metal band.' Actually that's quite hard to do, especially for a large device like the iPhone. So, we'll drop one star from our rating and carry on with the review.

So, if you can handle the high cost and the signal problem you'll want to know what you get for your money. Well, what you get is a very high quality device that's approximately the same height and width as the previous iPhone, but considerably slimmer, at just 9.3mm thick. It still weighs in at a chunky 137g though. It smells of quality, of course, from the box to the accessories, to the device itself, but apart from the slimness it doesn't look very different to previous iPhones.

The display is the same size as previous iPhones at 3.5 inches, but the new display packs in double the number of pixels in each direction, giving a total of 960 x 640 pixels and fantastic image quality as a result.

Apart from the screen, the biggest change comes in the form of upgraded cameras. The still camera has been given a larger sensor so it takes better images at night and in low light, the resolution has been increased to 5 megapixels and an LED flash added. The video camera has been seriously uprated to record videos at HD resolution (720p). Note that you can only make video calls to other iPhone 4 users and only on Wi-Fi. That's rather limiting.

The other main improvement is the battery life of the phone. Although the quoted standby time is the same, Apple say that talktime and web browsing time have been improved by around 40%.

So, Apple have created one of the very best phones on the market, but potentially a flawed beauty. Does it work as a phone? Not if you have no signal! But there are ways to work around that if you really want to. Is it worth the money? Is it worth the risk? Only you can decide.

2 Read the grade descriptions on page vii and then write your answer to the exam question.

_____

_____

_____

_____

_____

_____

_____

_____

_____

_____

_____

_____

_____

_____

_____

_____

_____

_____

RAISE MY GRADE

Skills to raise my grade

Now you have completed this lesson on comparison of texts, it's time to fill in the RAG table below to see if your confidence has improved.

	R	A	G
I understand which questions want me to focus on two different texts.	○	○	○
I can understand what these questions are asking me to do.	○	○	○
I can confidently handle two texts and know how to use the material to answer questions.	○	○	○
I can use the evidence from the texts to support my ideas when comparing/evaluating texts.	○	○	○
I know how to organise my answer, making sure I write chronologically, coherently and use both texts.	○	○	○

2 Writing information and ideas

Before you start

When you are planning your writing, it is important that you concentrate on the following:

Audience and Style	This is the person or people that you are writing for or to. In the exam, you need to work out the audience for your writing because this will help you work out how to write. For example, if you are writing a letter to a friend or relation, you will be friendly and informal. If you are writing a report for a school governor, you will need to be more serious and formal.
Purpose	This is *why* you are writing. In the exam you need to work out the purpose or reason for your writing to help you work out what you need to do/include. For example, the purpose may be to give information to another person or it may be to persuade someone to do something.
Format	This is the way that you set out your writing. It is important that you know what the different types of writing look like. For example, a formal letter or a report will be set out very differently from an informal letter or a review. This is something you can revise and learn before the exam.
Content	Once you have worked out exactly what you are doing, who it is for and what it needs to look like, then you can think about the content – or what you are going to include.

Content and organisation (13 marks)

A grade answer

(10–13 marks)

- You show a sophisticated understanding of the purpose of the task.
- You have a sustained awareness of the reader.
- Your coverage is well judged and detailed.
- Your points are convincingly developed.
- You use paragraphs to enhance your writing.
- You have a sophisticated range of stylistic devices.
- You use appropriate and ambitious vocabulary.

C grade answer

(7–9 marks)

- You know exactly what you are being asked to do in your writing.
- You know exactly who you are writing for and have thought about what will interest that person or group.
- Your work is long enough and you have covered a number of points in detail.
- Your writing has paragraphs and the structure of your writing makes your ideas clear.
- You have used a good variety of carefully chosen words.
- You have thought carefully about why you are writing and who you are writing for, and have adapted your style to suit them.
- You have got all the details of the appropriate audience correct.

Sentence structure, content and spelling *(7 marks)*

7 Informal letters

Skills to raise my grade

Fill in the RAG table below to show how confident you are in the following areas:

	R	A	G
I know when I am being asked to produce an informal letter.	○	○	○
I know how to prepare for informal letters (thinking about audience, purpose, format and content).	○	○	○
I understand how to structure an informal letter.	○	○	○
I am confident that I know what to include in an informal letter.	○	○	○
I understand how my work will be assessed.	○	○	○

Informal letters are usually written to someone you know fairly well (like a friend or relation) and the level of formality that you use will depend on how well you know them. You are likely to write a better letter if you address it to someone that you actually know instead of an imaginary person.

The way you start and end your letter will be a clear clue to the examiner that you have understood that you are writing an informal letter. It is very important that you avoid using the text language or slang that you might use with your friends – remember, you are still being assessed on your ability to write clearly and correctly.

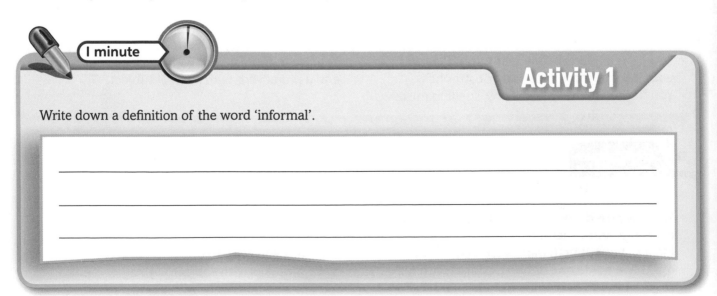

I minute

Activity 1

Write down a definition of the word 'informal'.

_____

_____

_____

3 minutes

Activity 2

Look at the different exam questions below and identify whether they are formal (F) or informal (I) letters.

Exam question	Formal or Informal?
Write a letter to a friend who is moving to your town.	
Your coat was stolen at a local restaurant. Write a letter of complaint.	
Your cousin has asked you to visit them in Australia. Write your letter in response.	
You are concerned about litter from the local school. Write a letter to the headteacher.	
Write a letter of application for a part-time job in a local café.	
Write to your MP about the lack of recycling facilities in your area.	
You are worried about a friend who is constantly tired. Write a letter advising them to seek some help.	

5 minutes

Activity 3

It is important to plan your letter before you write your exam answer. Look at the exam question below.

You have a friend who has decided to do a bungee jump for their birthday. Write a letter to your friend, giving your thoughts about their decision. *(20 marks)*

Complete the following planning exercise.

Audience _____

Purpose _____

Format _____

Content (what you will include)

_____

_____

_____

_____

_____

_____

20 minutes

Activity 4

Read the grade descriptions on pages 48–9, then write your answer to the exam question in Activity 3. Refer back to the grade descriptions as you write.

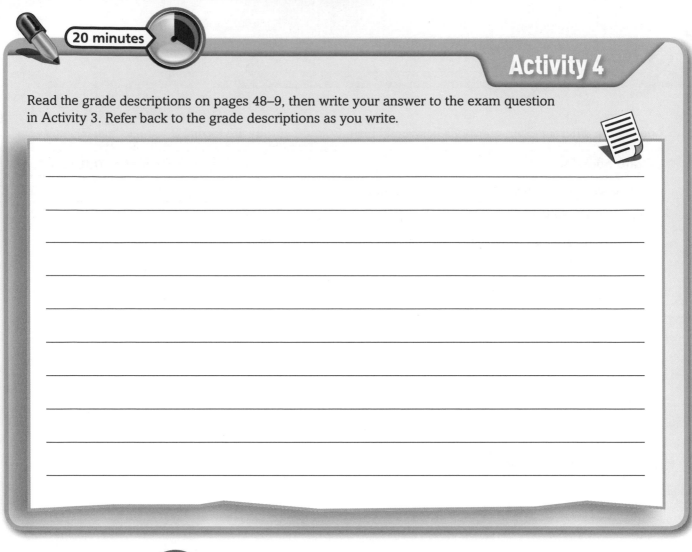

_____

_____

_____

_____

_____

_____

_____

_____

_____

5 minutes

Activity 5

You will now be given the opportunity to review and assess your work.

1 Look back at the informal letter you have written and check your answer against this success criteria table. Tick any of the essential features that you have included.

	✓ or ✗
A clear address	
A date	
A clear greeting that is suitable for a friend	
My writing is paragraphed	
Each paragraph begins with a different opening/they are well linked	
My writing is sentenced and each sentence is punctuated	
My writing has a clear concluding paragraph	
My letter ends with a closing phrase	
My letter is long enough	

2 Using the grade descriptions on pages 48–9, which grade have you achieved? ⬜

Read the following exam question, then look closely at the student answers to the question given below.

> You have a friend or relative who has recently moved to a foreign country.
> You decide to write to them to see how they are coping. *(20 marks)*

Student 1

Used the correct format for a letter

Identified the correct audience

Used an informal tone

Arranged into paragraphs

Sensible order of ideas

Varied the beginnings of some sentences

> 16 Sparky Lane
> Bexley
> 16.06.2011
>
> Hi Beth,
> What's going on with you these days? I heared you moved
> to Spain from my mum's sister and I can't believe you
> actualy went ahed and did it. I now you have been talking
> aboat it for ages now and I say good for you. I can still
> rememmber how much you luved Spanish lessons or was it
> just Mr Bancroft that you luved? Haha, we used to luv his
> lessons didn't we?
>
> Anyway, what's it like over their? How are you enjoying the
> food? What's the whether bin like since you got their? The
> fourcast says that it has been better than over here as
> we only seem to have had rain all them time this summer.
> Wile I'm on about the whether, have you had many spiders?
> I know they like the hot weather and I know you could never
> cope very well with creepie cralies. Do you get insect bites
> very much?

1 Look at the features of grade C writing that are in boxes surrounding Student 1's letter.
   See if you can draw an arrow between the feature in the box and where you can see that
   feature in the student's writing. Can you also highlight any spelling mistakes in their work?
2 Remind yourself of the grade descriptions on pages 48–9.
   Do you think Student 1 has managed to achieve a grade C?

Examiner comment 1

Despite a clear sense of relationship and a pleasant, friendly tone, the content was fairly limited. The student's spelling and grammatical issues detract from the writing. There are far too many spelling errors and homophones are an issue. The letter is too short, and has no conclusion.

Now read Student 2's answer. This is an extract from a longer letter written in response to the exam question on page 53.

Firm grasp of audience

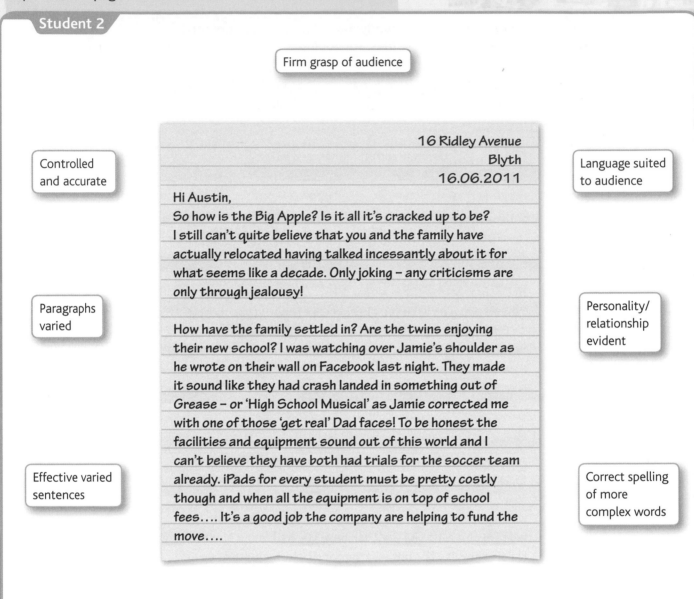

16 Ridley Avenue
Blyth
16.06.2011

Hi Austin,
So how is the Big Apple? Is it all it's cracked up to be?
I still can't quite believe that you and the family have
actually relocated having talked incessantly about it for
what seems like a decade. Only joking – any criticisms are
only through jealousy!

How have the family settled in? Are the twins enjoying
their new school? I was watching over Jamie's shoulder as
he wrote on their wall on Facebook last night. They made
it sound like they had crash landed in something out of
Grease – or 'High School Musical' as Jamie corrected me
with one of those 'get real' Dad faces! To be honest the
facilities and equipment sound out of this world and I
can't believe they have both had trials for the soccer team
already. iPads for every student must be pretty costly
though and when all the equipment is on top of school
fees…. It's a good job the company are helping to fund the
move….

Controlled and accurate

Paragraphs varied

Effective varied sentences

Language suited to audience

Personality/ relationship evident

Correct spelling of more complex words

Punctuation is varied and effective

3 Look at the features of grade A writing that are in boxes surrounding Student 2's letter.
   See if you can draw an arrow between the feature in the box and where you can see that
   feature in the student's writing.

Examiner comment 2

The letter is appropriately structured with a clear opening paragraph where the student manages to effortlessly demonstrate to the examiner that they have an existing relationship with 'Austin'. The writing is well-controlled and sentences are varied, creating an easygoing and natural sounding informal letter. Writing is accurately punctuated with some varied punctuation evident.

4 Now think about the differences between the two letters you have just read. Write down
   three differences between a strong answer and an answer that needs development. Use these as
   tips when you write your next informal letter.

_____

_____

_____

_____

_____

_____

_____

_____

_____

_____

_____

_____

_____

Skills to raise my grade

RAISE MY GRADE

Now you have completed this lesson on informal letters,
it's time to fill in the RAG table below to see if your confidence
has improved.

	R	A	G
I know when I am being asked to produce an informal letter.	○	○	○
I know how to prepare for informal letters (thinking about audience, purpose, format and content).	○	○	○
I understand how to structure an informal letter.	○	○	○
I am confident that I know what to include in an informal letter.	○	○	○
I understand how my work will be assessed.	○	○	○

8 Formal letters

Skills you need ▶

You must show that you can:
- recognise when you are being asked to write a formal letter
- structure a formal letter
- understand what to include in a formal letter

Skills to raise my grade

RAISE MY GRADE

Fill in the RAG table below to show how confident you are in the following areas:

	R	A	G
I know when I am being asked to produce a formal letter.	○	○	○
I know how to prepare for formal letters (thinking about audience, purpose, format and content).	○	○	○
I understand how to structure a formal letter.	○	○	○
I am confident that I know what to include in a formal letter.	○	○	○
I understand how my work will be assessed.	○	○	○

Formal letters are usually written to someone you are not overly familiar with and can be written for a number of different reasons. You might wish to persuade someone to do something, you might want to make a complaint or you may wish to give information to someone.

It is essential that you revise the layout and writing conventions for formal letter writing, and make sure you follow the task while sustaining a formal tone and style.

3 minutes

Activity 1

1 Below you will see a list of possible letter salutations (opening greetings). Only **two** of these should be used for formal letters. Highlight the two correct formal letter salutations.

2 Look across the page and highlight the **two** correct ways to close a formal letter. Draw an arrow to match the correct formal salutation and formal letter closure.

Possible salutations:	**Possible letter closings:**
Hi James,	Yours faithfully
Alright,	See you
Dear Sir or Madam,	Love
Dearest Helen,	Yours sincerely
Dear Mr Jones,	Take care

6 minutes

One way to improve the quality of your written work is to think about how you begin your sentences. Many students tend to use the same openings throughout their work. This becomes repetitive and so detracts from the quality of their writing.

Look at the following paragraph. It is an extract from a letter about changing the school day. Improve the sentence openings by adding your changes in the table below. The first one has been done for you.

I have recently heard about your decision to alter the school day and I have to say that I am disgusted. I have heard about a number of other schools in the local area who have experimented with a similar system and all have now reverted to their original school hours. I think this should clearly indicate the fact that it was not a success.

I do want to stress that I am very unhappy.

I am worried about my children. I do think that if school starts at 8.00am then in the winter they will be walking to school in the dark. I also feel that they will be less visible to drivers. I have a neighbour whose son does a paper round and he will be unable to work if the change goes ahead.

Sentence opening	Your changes
I have recently heard…	Recently I heard about your decision…
I have heard…	
I think this should…	
I am worried…	
I do think…	
I also feel that…	
I have a neighbour…	

25 minutes

Read the exam question below.

> **You recently went out for a meal with some friends for your birthday. The service was poor, the food was terrible and the table was dirty. You felt that the evening went so badly that it ruined your birthday. Write a letter of complaint to the manager, explaining exactly what happened and what you expect them to do.** *(20 marks)*

Complete the following planning exercise.

Audience _____ **Purpose** _____

Format _____

Content (what you will include) _____

_____

_____

Now write your own letter in response to this exam question.

_____
_____
_____
_____
_____
_____
_____
_____
_____
_____
_____
_____
_____

10 minutes

Activity 4

Read the two student answers to the exam question in Activity 3. Both answers have been written in response to the same exam question, but one is stronger than the other.

Student 1

Mr Jones	22 Oakland Way
Buena Restaurant	Leeds
Leeds	LS12 2BB
LS12 5XF	22 Jan 2011

Dear Mr Jones,

Over the years, your restaurant has been a firm favourite with our family. Numerous birthdays have been held in the restaurant in addition to the occasional Christmas celebration and frequent meals out at weekends. It saddens me to write this letter but last weekend was my dear wife's 60th and to put it mildly we were utterly appalled.

We do not mind having to wait to be seated and usually have an aperitif in the bar prior to our meal, in fact this is something we enjoy. However, the bar was being stocked and a rather rude young man told us we would have to 'wait 'til I'm done.' We waited. And we waited. After almost 25 minutes he reluctantly brought over two gin and tonics in chipped glasses with no ice, the wrong bottle of wine and to top it off he had completely forgotten the beers. But this was just the start of our problems.

The table was badly set on a somewhat grey and dishevelled looking table cloth, the cutlery was encrusted with small particles of food, the wines glasses were covered in finger prints and the flowers were dead. The menus were sticky and the 'new and improved menu' that we had been eagerly awaiting was little more than a 75% reduction of the normal menu in terms of choice but a 75% increase in terms of cost. Determined not to ruin my wife's birthday we set about ordering with great enthusiasm. Our enthusiasm was met by a monosyllabic teenager called Sam (unfortunately their gender was unclear as most of their face was under a mop of greasy hair) who stonily told us that most of our choices were unavailable, so we ordered 8 portions of fish and chips.

The fish was cold. The plates were cold. The chips were cold. It was truly awful. We didn't even bother with a pudding and instead hurried out of the door (leaving no tip much to Sam's audible disgust) and fled into the working men's club next door. Not our normal choice – but at least we were able to get a decent drink and a few packets of crisps.

I seriously suggest you investigate the contents of this letter. I expect a full refund but more than that, I would like to see the staff, the décor, the cleanliness and the wonderful food to be restored to its usual standard.

Yours sincerely,
Philip Matthews

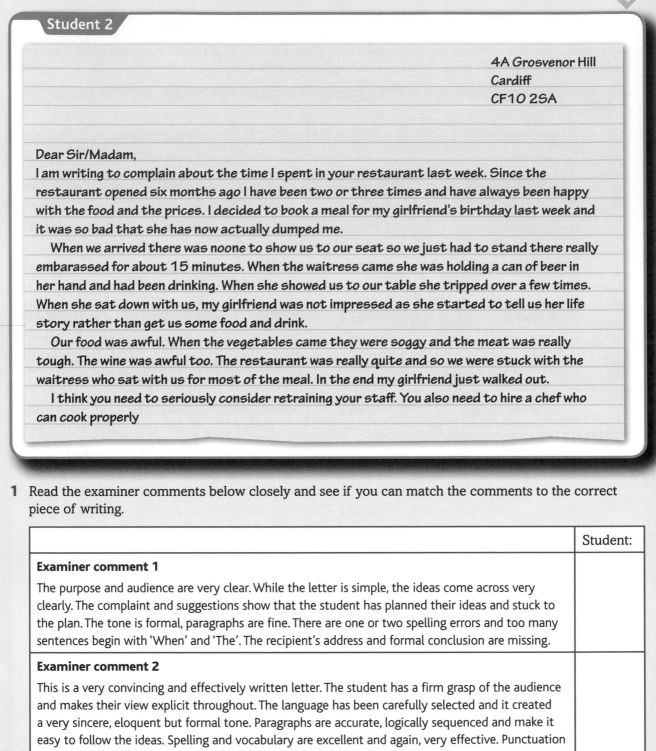

Student 2

4A Grosvenor Hill
Cardiff
CF10 2SA

Dear Sir/Madam,

I am writing to complain about the time I spent in your restaurant last week. Since the restaurant opened six months ago I have been two or three times and have always been happy with the food and the prices. I decided to book a meal for my girlfriend's birthday last week and it was so bad that she has now actually dumped me.

When we arrived there was noone to show us to our seat so we just had to stand there really embarassed for about 15 minutes. When the waitress came she was holding a can of beer in her hand and had been drinking. When she showed us to our table she tripped over a few times. When she sat down with us, my girlfriend was not impressed as she started to tell us her life story rather than get us some food and drink.

Our food was awful. When the vegetables came they were soggy and the meat was really tough. The wine was awful too. The restaurant was really quite and so we were stuck with the waitress who sat with us for most of the meal. In the end my girlfriend just walked out.

I think you need to seriously consider retraining your staff. You also need to hire a chef who can cook properly

1 Read the examiner comments below closely and see if you can match the comments to the correct piece of writing.

	Student:
Examiner comment 1 The purpose and audience are very clear. While the letter is simple, the ideas come across very clearly. The complaint and suggestions show that the student has planned their ideas and stuck to the plan. The tone is formal, paragraphs are fine. There are one or two spelling errors and too many sentences begin with 'When' and 'The'. The recipient's address and formal conclusion are missing.	
Examiner comment 2 This is a very convincing and effectively written letter. The student has a firm grasp of the audience and makes their view explicit throughout. The language has been carefully selected and it created a very sincere, eloquent but formal tone. Paragraphs are accurate, logically sequenced and make it easy to follow the ideas. Spelling and vocabulary are excellent and again, very effective. Punctuation is competent and varied.	

2 Write down **three** things that you could do to improve the grade of Student 2's answer.

5 minutes

Activity 5

1 Look back at the letter you wrote in Activity 3. Think about what you have done so far this lesson and write down two things that you feel you have done well and two things that you need to improve in your next letter.

- _____
- _____
- _____
- _____

2 Look at each of the assessment criteria for grade C and grade A in the checklist below. Tick where you see the criteria demonstrated in your work.

Assessment checklist

Have I achieved a grade C?	✓/✗	Have I achieved a grade A?	✓/✗
I have identified the correct audience		I have appealed to and engaged my audience	
I have used the correct format for my letter		My format and structure are effective	
I have used a formal tone throughout		I have crafted my tone/language for the audience	
I have arranged my writing into paragraphs		My paragraphs are varied in length and structure	
The order of my ideas follows the task and my letter is long enough		My writing has detail and is well developed, being of a suitable length for the task	
My ideas are clear and I have added detail		My vocabulary is varied, effective and extended	
I have varied the beginnings of some sentences		I effectively vary sentences throughout	
My spelling is mostly accurate		My spelling is correct	
My punctuation is varied and mostly accurate		My punctuation is varied and effective	
		My tone and overall explanation are very convincing	

GradeStudio

Read the following examination question. Spend no more than two minutes planning your answer.

You see the following comment in a newspaper.

'Technology is killing the children of today. All they can think about are mobile phones, Facebook, games consoles, computers, TV programmes and so on. Any decent parent should limit the use of these to one hour per day.'

You feel very strongly about the writer's views. Write your answer to the editor of the newspaper.

(20 marks)

Now write your answer. Remember to refer to the grade descriptions on pages 48–9 before you begin and throughout your writing time.

_____

_____

_____

_____

_____

_____

_____

_____

_____

_____

_____

_____

Once you have completed your answer you can refer back to the checklist on page 61 and tick the features you have included in your own work to see how well you have done.

RAISE MY GRADE

Skills to raise my grade

Now you have completed this lesson on formal letters, it's time to fill in the RAG table below to see if your confidence has improved.

	R	A	G
I know when I am being asked to produce a formal letter.	○	○	○
I know how to prepare for formal letters (thinking about audience, purpose, format and content).	○	○	○
I understand how to structure a formal letter.	○	○	○
I am confident that I know what to include in a formal letter.	○	○	○
I understand how my work will be assessed.	○	○	○

9 Reports

Skills you need ▶

You must show that you can:
- recognise when you are being asked to write a report
- structure a report
- understand what to include in a report

Skills to raise my grade

RAISE MY GRADE ↑

Fill in the RAG table below to show how confident you are in the following areas:	R	A	G
I know when I am being asked to produce a report.	○	○	○
I know how to prepare for reports (thinking about audience, purpose, format and content).	○	○	○
I understand how to structure a report.	○	○	○
I am confident that I know what to include in a report.	○	○	○
I understand how my work will be assessed.	○	○	○

A report is a formal document that follows a specific format. These documents aim to give advice, outline issues and then give potential solutions regarding what can be done about them.

When you are writing a report it is important that you organise and present your ideas sensibly and clearly so that your main concerns are very clear to your audience. The tone of your report should be respectful – you are offering information and views, so if you want your audience to listen to your ideas, you must sound professional and knowledgeable.

3 minutes

Activity 1

1 Explain what a report is.

_____

_____

_____

_____

2 What might you be asked to write a report on?

_____

_____

_____

_____

_____

_____

2 minutes

Activity 2

1 Number the following features of a report 1–5 in the order in which you should see them.

A concluding paragraph giving recommendations about what should happen next.	
Signature/title of the person writing the report and the date of the report.	
A brief introduction to show why you are writing the report.	
A clear title establishing the audience and purpose.	
Paragraphs, each with a subheading, containing your different ideas.	

2 Now look at the statements about reports below and identify whether they are true or false.

	True or False
Conclusions should summarise your findings and make recommendations.	
You need to set out your report like a letter.	
The purpose of a report is often to entertain your reader.	
Use subheadings to make each different section clear.	
Reports use informal language so the writing is easy to understand.	
Pictures should be used in reports to illustrate what you are talking about.	
Include a brief introduction outlining why you are writing the report.	
You should use as many complicated words as possible to get the top grade.	
A report needs a clear title making the audience and the purpose clear.	
Your report should be between one and two pages in length.	
You should include your name and signature and the date of the report.	

5 minutes

Activity 3

Homophones are words which sound the same but are spelled differently, for example wear/where. The following paragraph taken from a report on school facilities is filled with homophone errors.

Highlight the errors in the text and write the correct spellings in the space around it.

At are school their are a huge number of issues with the facilities. They're are to many problems with the school jim. Most of the time we have to use the school fields but when the whether is bad we have to use the gym. For starters, the plaice is an absolute mess. When you go threw the door, you are encouraged not to where you're trainers in the gym to save the floors but the wooden floor is bearly safe as the wood has become filled with splinters and cracks. This is shocking as the floor is farely knew as it was only put in three years ago.

Another plaice that concerns me is the changing rooms. There is one peace of the wall that has a huge gap in it. Not only does this cause drafts in the winter but people can stair through when your getting changed. We are not aloud to cover the whole as the PE staff claim we could cause more damage.

5 minutes

Activity 4

Read the following exam question.

The governors at your school are considering selling the school fields to a builder who wants to use the space to build 50 houses. The money raised from the sale of the fields would be used to build a new computer suite, but many PE lessons would have to take place in the school hall and the school canteen.

You have been asked to write a report about the proposal above. *(20 marks)*

Taking time to plan your writing is a crucial part of report writing. Write down what you would include in your report using the space below.

_____

_____

_____

_____

25 minutes

Activity 5

Now you need to write the answer you have planned to the exam question in Activity 4.
Below are some tips to help you get started.

- Make sure you begin by giving your report a title which clearly states the purpose of the report and who it is written for.
- Keep your introduction very short with only an outline of your concerns.
- Use subheadings to make it clear what you are writing about.
- Write a clear conclusion where you summarise the main points and include any recommendations.
- Maintain formal language and a formal style and tone in your report.

5 minutes

Activity 6

1 You will now be given the opportunity to review and assess your work. Reflect on your answer using the assessment checklist below. You should tick the areas where you think you have met the criteria.

Assessment checklist

Have I achieved a grade C?	✓ / ✗	Example in my work
I have identified the correct audience in my clear title		
I have used the correct format for my report		
I have used a formal tone throughout		
I have arranged my writing into paragraphs with subheadings		
The order of my ideas follows the task and my letter is long enough		
My ideas are clear and I have added detail		
I have varied the beginnings of some sentences		
My spelling is mostly accurate		
My punctuation is varied and mostly accurate		

Have I achieved a grade A?	✓ / ✗	Example in my work
I have appealed to and engaged my audience		
My format and structure are effective and accurate		
I have crafted my tone/language for the audience		
My paragraphs are varied in length and structure		
My writing has detail and is well developed, being of a suitable length for the task		
I effectively vary sentences throughout		
My spelling is correct		
My vocabulary is varied, effective and extended		
My punctuation is varied and effective		
My tone and overall explanation is very convincing		

Read the following exam question.

> **Your friend was involved in an accident in a science lesson. You feel that the room is very unsafe and have decided to write a report for the headteacher, outlining your concerns and suggesting what should be done to improve the facilities.**
>
> *(20 marks)*

Read the student answer below.

C grade answer

Student 1

A report to the head teacher on *Redcar School's* Science Rooms

Introduction

There was an accident in our science lesson last week. A boy burnt his arm owing to the faulty Bunsen burners and the wonky floors. I think that the science labs are becoming too dangerous and something needs to be done to stop anymore from happening.

Problems with the facilities

The rooms are not safe. The benches that we sit on are very wobbly because of the legs and this makes us wobble around during experiments. The roof leaks in more than one place and this makes pretty big puddles on the floor which is also very dangerous as the floors are uneven so you get quite big puddles when it is raining heavily.

Problems with the equipment

The equipment is awful. The Bunsen burner gas taps are loose so they can be turned on very easily even if they are knocked by a pencil case. The gas pipes are also worn so we often get gas leaks which is very dangerous. The tripods that go over the burners are all wonky so the experiments and chemicals often fall over. The beakers are cracked and there is no lock on the chemical cupboard which is very dangerous.

Recommendations

I think we need to spend some money on the building to make it safer for now but in the long term we need to save some money and build new labs. We could spend some of the money from the sponsored walk last month and buy new glass tubes and beakers and charge students money if they break them. We need to turn the gas off completely until the pipes and taps are fixed.

Examiner comment

This student has worked hard on their format so the report is professional, clear and logical for the reader. There are some long sentences which need breaking down. Some of the ideas could benefit from added detail and explanation. Spelling is fine but they could work on vocabulary and need to remove words like 'wonky'. There is some repetition, e.g. 'dangerous' which is due to lack of vocabulary rather than deliberate effect. The student has not concluded the report appropriately. It should have a signature and a date. A grade C was awarded.

1 Write down **two** things that the student does well and **two** things that the student needs to improve.

Two things that the student does well:

- _____

- _____

Two things that the student needs to improve:

- _____

- _____

2 Look at the highlighted phrases in the student's answer and see if you can improve them. You should focus on punctuation, sentencing and clarifying the detail within the sentence.

Write your improvements in the space around the report.

This next report on the opposite page has been written by a student from the same school, but they have expanded on a number of the points and issues. Look closely at their work opposite.

3 Highlight the sentences/words/phrases that you feel contribute towards their grade A. Use the grade A criteria in the assessment checklist on page 68 to guide you.

4 Using the grade A criteria, write the examiner comment for this answer.

_____

_____

_____

_____

_____

_____

Student 2

For the Attention of: The Head teacher
Problems relating to *Redcar School's Science Rooms*

Introduction
Last week we fortunately avoided a very serious accident when a faulty Bunsen burner exploded in a classroom. This is the fifth accident this academic year and it is only a matter of time before others are permanently damaged. The laboratories were built as a temporary building solution almost thirty years ago and they have ceased to be an effective teaching facility and are simply a serious hazard.

Problems with the facilities
The class rooms are unsafe. From the faulty wiring in the light sockets (which often turn themselves off or flicker during bad weather) to the leaking roof (which as you know creates a hazardously slippery floor); the rooms are not fit for students or teachers. The benches are also particularly dangerous, not least because they are worn and cracked but because the legs are uneven causing students to perch precariously on the edge which means we are uncomfortable and vulnerable to accidents.

Problems with the equipment
The equipment is simply appalling. Most Bunsen burner gas taps are so loose that they are frequently switched on during lessons when knocked, this causes the classroom to smell but the continuous gas in the room must be a fire hazard. The gas pipes are also perished which contributes to further gas leaks in the laboratory. Uneven tripods, cracked beakers and test tubes and a general lack of safety equipment all contribute to the danger in our lessons. A chemical cupboard is potentially the most dangerous item in a school. With no lock, students have easy access to a wide range of lethal chemicals that could not only cause damage to students (if in the wrong hands) but damage to the school itself.

Recommendations
In the short term, the school needs to seriously consider the future of these classrooms. Personally, I would close them with immediate effect to prevent any further incidents. We also need to focus on the safety aspects of the lessons. Purchasing safety goggles and new glass ware for experiment will increase the safety of experiments. No lock on the chemical cupboard is a disaster waiting to happen, a problem that should be rectified with immediate effect.
Lisa Cooke
22nd February 2011

Skills to raise my grade

Now you have completed this lesson on reports, it's time to fill in the RAG table below to see if your confidence has improved.

	R	A	G
I know when I am being asked to produce a report.	○	○	○
I know how to prepare for reports (thinking about audience, purpose, format and content).	○	○	○
I understand how to structure a report.	○	○	○
I am confident that I know what to include in a report.	○	○	○
I understand how my work will be assessed.	○	○	○

10 Articles

Skills to raise my grade

Fill in the RAG table below to show how confident you are in the following areas:

	R	A	G
I understand when I am being asked to produce an article.	○	○	○
I know how to prepare for articles (thinking about audience, purpose, format and content).	○	○	○
I understand how to structure an article.	○	○	○
I am confident that I know what to include in an article.	○	○	○
I understand how my work will be assessed.	○	○	○

Articles are documents that discuss news or items of general interest to a specific group of people. Articles can be written for a number of different reasons, for example, to entertain people, to inform or to persuade.

In the exam you are being assessed for your ability to write an article for a given purpose and audience. Do not worry about including pictures – you are assessed on your ability to write. If you are asked to write for a teenage audience, you might be less formal and include some humour, but it is important that you do not use slang or text language.

5 minutes

Activity 1

Writers can use a range of different features to make their writing interesting. Opposite is a table of features, their definition and an example of each in use. Some of the boxes have been left empty. Complete the table using the list below.

A play on words – often used in titles	To order or command
Emotive language	A question where the answer is obvious
You must donate now	Sarcasm
I mean, it's just not meant to happen that way	Alliteration
Exaggeration	

Features	Definition	Example
Rhetorical questions		How many of us have walked past a homeless person and pretended not to see them?
Ellipsis	… builds suspense/shows there is more to say	The boy was utterly rejected and had nowhere to go…
Second person direct appeal	Use of 'you' to make the reader feel involved	
	Suggesting something is better than it actually is	The new X-Box 750 is better than life itself!
First person plural	'We' suggests a sense of unity/ the reader has something in common with the writer	We can fight racism together
	To ridicule or mock someone/ something by saying the opposite of what you mean	People who are cruel to animals must be so proud of themselves
Imperatives		Imagine a resort where the blue sea stretches as far as you can see
	Words beginning with the same letter	Endless emotion engulfed the viewers
Pun		I've failed the mathematics test so many times I've lost count
	Words that appeal to our feelings	The floods were catastrophic, ruthless and unrelenting
Informal tone (where appropriate)	Deliberately relaxed language to make the reader feel at ease	

5 minutes

Activity 2

1 Read the introduction to an article below. Highlight any features that the writer has used to engage the reader.

Does this sound familiar? Can you relate to this? They don't listen properly, don't eat regularly and never stop chatting on the phone? I'm not talking about tearaway, troublesome teenagers, I'm talking about my mum. Trust me, we teenagers have terrible reputations for pretty much everything but my mum doesn't seem to accept that most of my bad habits come from her.

OK, so she has a busy life. But so do we all. What we don't need to hear is how much she has to do about 7 million times a day. And doesn't she do it so quietly? Cleaned your room, washed the hall carpet, walked the dog, and bathed the goldfish… honestly what does she want, a medal?

Then there's her discipline. Can I really compare her to a prison warden? Yes I can. It's all, 'Do this!', 'Don't do that'. Don't get me wrong, I love my mum to bits but I wish she was a little more knowing and a little less no-ing!

2 Look back at the introduction on page 73. Complete the table below by writing down one example of each of the features you found in the introduction.

Feature	Example from the text
Rhetorical questions	
Ellipsis	
Second person direct appeal	
Exaggeration	
First person plural	
Sarcasm	
Imperatives	
Alliteration	
Pun	
Emotive language	
Informal tone (where appropriate)	

3 Can you see any other features not mentioned in the table? Add them to the table and remember to write down the example from the text.

4 What effect might the use of all these features have on the reader of the article?

_____

_____

_____

_____

_____

_____

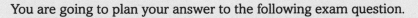

5 minutes

Activity 3

You are going to plan your answer to the following exam question.

Write an article for a teenage magazine about a person you either admire or dislike.

(20 marks)

The first thing you need to do is to think about the format of your article.

A suggested structure for the format of your article is included below, with some advice about what you should include at each stage.

Use the planning space to write down what you will include in each section to answer the exam question above.

Format of an article	Article plan
Headline or article title • Keep it short • Make it catchy • Give an idea of what the rest of the article will be about	
Introduction of the article • Give a brief outline of the subject of the article • Keep this section to a few initial ideas and sentences	
Main body of the article • Try to answer all the reader's questions like 'why', 'how' and 'what' • Make each paragraph relevant to the subject or the title of the article • Add plenty of detail so your reader fully understands you • Answer the important points in this section	
Conclusion of the article • This should be at the end of your article • Give a summary of the article in brief • Give recommendations/an overview and a catchy ending	

Often a task will specify a specific tone (i.e. lively) and this may encourage you to entertain the reader using a range of humorous devices and statements. Do read the task carefully, as you may be asked to write about a serious topic where humour is not appropriate.

GradeStudio

Below are two extracts from two students' articles, written in answer to the exam question in Activity 3.

1 Highlight any words and phrases that suggest to you how the students feel about Melanie Jones and James Corden.

2 Look at the two examiner comments that follow the student answers. Match the examiner comments to the students' articles.

Explain why you have chosen the comments to match the articles.

Student	Examiner comment	Why they match
1		
2		

Student 1

Love her or hate her, Melanie Jones is one of the most photographed and talked about women in the United Kingdom, on a weekly basis. Think about it, when was the last time you cast your eye over the magazine counter in your local shop and did not see a picture of that unmistakable face pouting back at you?

I'll admit it, I don't know her as a person, I don't know what she is like as a mum and I certainly don't care who she is married to or if she's having another baby but, if I'm honest, I can't stand the woman.

Let's begin with the most obvious thing about her (and I don't mean the colossal shoes, the huge rear or the large shaggy mop). No, what I don't like is her mouth. Every time the woman is quoted I wish she would shut up. Everything she mutters is utterly lewd. She is clueless about ordinary people and how some of us struggle to make ends meet and thinks that it is perfectly acceptable to brag about how many fans she has and how many pairs of shoes she has bought each day. If I was her I'd spend my money going to etiquette and elocution lessons so she could learn how to speak in a slightly more human manner.

Next, onto the woman's clothes. Melanie Jones is a millionaire, so why does she dress like she has bought something 3 sizes too small for less than one pound? If it's lycra, she'll wear it, if it's tight she'll wear it and if it shows off most of her very plastic body then she'll wear it. Mel, why don't you look at Mrs Beckham – like her or not, she is one of the best dressed women in the world and has bagged (and held onto) without doubt the most fanciable hubby. As for yours…well, don't get me started…

Student 2

James Kimberley Corden has too be the funniest man on the TV at the moment. Every time I look at him he makes me smile and it's not the things he says, it's just the way that he looks like he is always having a bit of fun and a bit of a laugh.

The first time I had heard of James Corden was when he was in Gavin and Stacey and that is one of the best comedies every made. Everything that smith said and did was so over the top that it made me laugh out loud. The way he treats his sister, his mum and Nessa is just brilliant. He even jokes around with gavin's mum like when he slaps her bum and because he is so cheeky and funny he can get away with it.

I think the work that he has done for charity has been brilliant to. When he did sport relief he pretended to be in bed with david Beckham and he was so serious about it. He also did some speeches for sports relief too and the way he was so passonate about sport and winning it was very funny to watch. I think the fact that he is not embarrassed about being a big fat man in leg warmers and tight shorts also adds to his funniness.

James Corden is a hero of humour and I think he fully deserves every award that he has won and a few more. Move over Peter Kay because James corden is here to stay.

Examiner comment 1

There are a few missing capitals for names that the candidate needs to address. Some of the sentences are rather long and need either breaking down into two sentences or they require added commas. There are a couple of homophone errors throughout the work, the candidate is a little unsure of the difference between too/to. The content is lively and the candidate has clearly given a lot of though to the ideas they have included. Grade C

Examiner comment 2

The candidate has a very strong opinion about their chosen celebrity and takes every opportunity to demonstrate their excellent range of punctuation. Vocabulary suits the task and has been deliberately selected to emphasise the very different aspects to this celebrity. Assured and confident, the candidate very subtly mentions the things they dislike in a rather eloquent and non offensive way – rather than being blunt about what they don't like. The tone is great and perfect for the magazine type. Grade A*

25 minutes

Activity 4

Now consider the exam question below.

'They ruin our lessons, they ruin our streets and they ruin our reputation. A few badly behaved teenagers are out of control and they ruin everything for the rest of us. We need to control tearaway teenagers before it's too late.'

You have been asked to write an article about 'badly behaved teenagers', the problems they cause and how they should be punished. *(20 marks)*

1 Refer to the grade descriptions on pages 48–9 and aim to meet as many of the criteria as you can to achieve the best possible grade. Use the space on the following pages to write your answers.

_____

_____

_____

_____

_____

_____

5 minutes

Activity 5

Check your answer alongside the grade descriptions on pages 48–9. Based on the features, content and accuracy of your writing, what grade would you award your answer?

Write down **two** tips that will help you to improve next time.

• _____

• _____

RAISE MY GRADE

Skills to raise my grade

Now you have completed this lesson on articles, it's time to fill in the RAG table below to see if your confidence has improved.

	R	A	G
I understand when I am being asked to produce an article.	○	○	○
I know how to prepare for articles (thinking about audience, purpose, format and content).	○	○	○
I understand how to structure an article.	○	○	○
I am confident that I know what to include in an article.	○	○	○
I understand how my work will be assessed.	○	○	○

11 Leaflets

Skills you need ▶

You must show that you can:
- recognise when you are being asked to write a leaflet
- structure a leaflet
- understand what to include in a leaflet

Skills to raise my grade

RAISE MY GRADE ↑

Fill in the RAG table below to show how confident you are in the following areas:	R	A	G
I know when I am being asked to produce a leaflet.	◯	◯	◯
I know how to prepare for leaflets (thinking about audience, purpose, format and content).	◯	◯	◯
I understand how to structure a leaflet.	◯	◯	◯
I am confident that I know what to include in a leaflet.	◯	◯	◯
I understand how my work will be assessed.	◯	◯	◯

Leaflets are widely used in the UK today. They can be found in many different places, but usually they have been produced either to give information to people or to persuade people to visit a certain place or buy a certain product.

Leaflets can vary considerably, from small black and white pieces of folded A5 paper to a much larger, glossy and colourful leaflet for something like a tourist attraction (for example a theme park).

When you are producing a leaflet in the exam, the examiner understands that you do not have time to produce something colourful and packed with pictures (remember, you gain no marks for this). Instead they will be assessing your ability to organise your writing like a leaflet and to write in a leaflet style – with correct punctuation and spelling. It is important to remember that you need to write enough for the examiner to be able to assess your writing skills.

3 minutes

Activity 1

Complete the mind map on page 81, thinking about **who** reads leaflets, **why** they are produced and **where** you might find them.

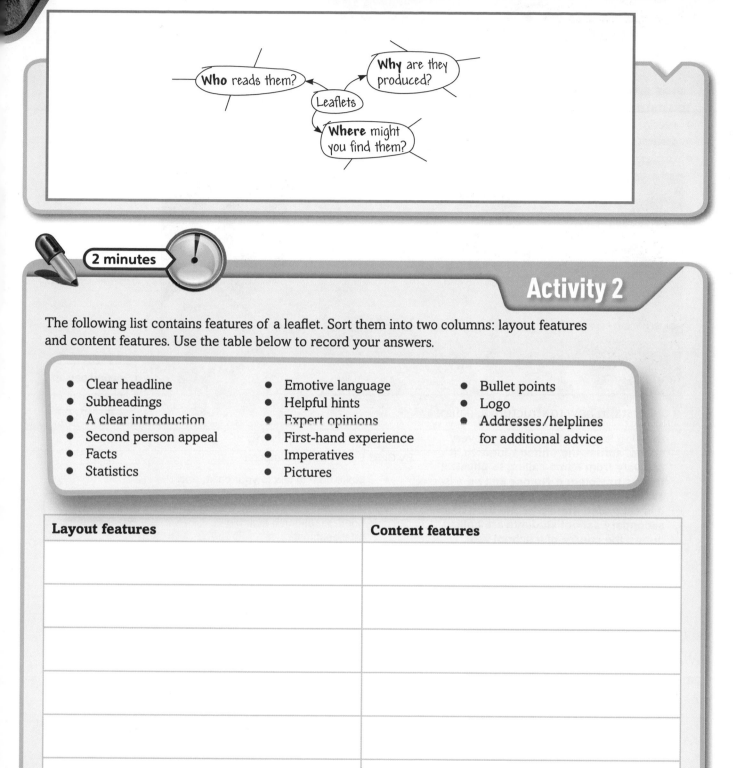

2 minutes

Activity 2

The following list contains features of a leaflet. Sort them into two columns: layout features and content features. Use the table below to record your answers.

- Clear headline
- Subheadings
- A clear introduction
- Second person appeal
- Facts
- Statistics
- Emotive language
- Helpful hints
- Expert opinions
- First-hand experience
- Imperatives
- Pictures
- Bullet points
- Logo
- Addresses/helplines for additional advice

Layout features	Content features

5 minutes

Activity 3

Look at the leaflet below. Draw arrows between the features and the appropriate sections of the leaflet.

Beating the Bullies – A Guide for Parents

Bullying is a problem in almost every school across the United Kingdom. It can vary from name-calling to physical threats to violence. No one knows exactly how much bullying goes on, but it is estimated that up to one third of all secondary school students are bullied during the course of a school year.

The facts
- Around 10% of children have missed school because of bullying
- Up to 40% of secondary school students feel that their teachers are unaware of bullying, even when it happens in the classroom
- About 17% of calls to ChildLine are about bullying. For five years running it has been the most common reason people call
- More 12-year-olds call ChildLine about bullying than any other age group

A case study
Jack's father feels bullying has changed his son from a happy boy to a frightened recluse:

'Bullying has changed my son completely. He used to be a popular and happy lad who loved school. Now he's so scared that he never goes out on an evening and he has to force himself to go to school every day. The teachers just don't seem to care…'

How to prevent bullying
By Child Expert Dr Ian Simpson

- Make time to talk to your child, and check that s/he is happy at school.
- Allow your child to bring friends home to reinforce suitable relationships.
- Make time to assist with class visits or help in class, so you can develop a more informed relationship with the class teacher and other students.
- NEVER openly criticise someone else's child's behaviour.
- Attend school open days and progress evenings so that you maintain a regular dialogue with the school.
- Give your child the opportunity to gain confidence and make a wide circle of friends by introducing him/her to after-school activities, e.g. sport, drama, music, etc.
- Give your child responsibility.

Extra help
- www.antibullying.net
- www.bullying.co.uk
- Childline: 08001111 or www. childline.org.uk

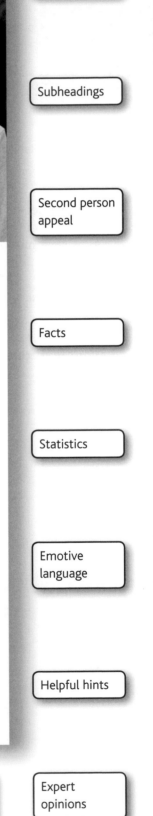

Clear headline

Subheadings

Second person appeal

Facts

Statistics

Emotive language

Helpful hints

Addresses/ helplines for additional advice

Pictures

Imperatives

First-hand experience

Expert opinions

30 minutes

Read the exam question below.

**Produce a leaflet persuading people to visit a tourist attraction in your area.
The attraction can be real or imaginary.**

(20 marks)

Complete the exam task above, remembering to include the following:

- a title
- an introduction to outline the tourist attraction
- information about the attractions and facilities
- open hours, price, travel, directions, etc.
- boxes with a description of the pictures that would be included.

5 minutes

Activity 5

You will now be given the opportunity to review and assess your work.

1 Spend two minutes going back through your work, checking for errors and amending any that you find.

2 Reflect on your work using the assessment checklist below. Tick the criteria that you feel you have achieved.

Assessment checklist

Have I achieved a grade C?	✓ or ✗
1 I have identified the correct audience in my clear title	
2 I have used the correct format for my leaflet	
3 I have used a persuasive tone throughout	
4 I have arranged my writing into paragraphs with headings where necessary	
5 The order of my ideas is sensible and helpful to the reader	
6 My ideas are clear and I have added detail	
7 I have varied the beginnings of some sentences	
8 My spelling is mostly accurate	
9 My punctuation is varied and mostly accurate	

Have I achieved a grade A?	✓ or ✗
1 I have constantly appealed to and engaged my audience	
2 My format and structure are effective and accurate	
3 I have crafted my tone/language for the audience	
4 My paragraphs are varied in length and structure	
5 My writing has detail and is well developed	
6 I effectively vary sentences throughout	
7 My spelling is correct	
8 My vocabulary is varied, effective and extended	
9 My punctuation is varied and effective	
10 My tone and overall explanation is very convincing	

3 Write down two tips that will help you improve next time.

- _____
- _____

10 minutes

The two student leaflets below and on page 86 have been given a grade by the examiner, but they have not been annotated and they do not have an overall examiner comment.

Read through each leaflet carefully, highlighting and jotting down where you feel the students have met the criteria in the assessment checklist on page 84. Then write a brief examiner comment in the comment boxes on page 87, to support the grade that the examiner has awarded.

C grade answer

Student 1

Diggerland

Introduction:

Diggerland is a great day out if you have a family. There are lots of Diggerland places all over the country but this one is in Durham. The aim of Diggerland is to have as much fun as possible in a Digger. It's for all the family and can be a really good way to spend an afternoon together. It is for all the family as each ride is a real machine that has been adapted to allow it to be driven by a 5 year old.

picture of big digger

What do you do?

Diggerland is pretty simple. You get in a digger with some safety equipment and then you go and drive over huge bumps of mud and sand. You get thrown all over the place and get up some decent speeds. Each park has many different rides and drives and these include

• Joyrider
• Digger Dodgems
• Go Karts
• Spindizzy
• Sky Shuttle
• Dumper Trucks
• Robots
• Dig-A-Round

Whos is for

Its for anyone who likes having a laugh with their family or their mates. Its not really good for under 5s as they can not drive the machines themselfes. It's really good for people who like a laugh and lots of people from buisinesses and even stag and hen dos like to go.

Prices

• Under 3 are free
• 3 to 65 is £17.00 per person
• Over 65's are £8.50

Diggerland is open all year round, even in the wet weather. So if you want a great day having fun then come to Diggerland and lets get digging!

A grade answer

Student 2

Bowland Wild Boar Park

Bowland Wild Boar Park is a 'must do' attraction for all animal and outdoor lovers. Situated approximately 2 miles from the picturesque village of Chipping and in the heart of the stunning Ribble Valley, Bowland Wild Boar Park has it all: dramatic weather fronts, dazzling scenery, luscious foliage and of course, an abundance of animals.

Farmer Jim
When you arrive you will be met by Farmer Jim... Behind the ruddy complexion, underneath the sarcasm and behind the false scowl you will quickly see why this venture has been a success. Farmer Jim runs the show and he does it perfectly. From the informative yet entertaining guided nature walk, the lamb feeding and barrel rides, Farmer Jim really knows how to engage the little ones. He'll have them cooing over the chicks and hiding in the haystack adventure before tiring them out on a trek.

Our Animals
At your own pace you can visit and feed the many animals, all of which look both healthy and happy in their oversized enclosures. Deer, llamas, goats, pigs, lambs, rabbits, wallabies, meerkats, the list is endless.

Attractions
When not visiting the animals the children can enjoy the pedal tractor area, tractor rides and superb play area with two very rapid zip slides! The adults can enjoy some local treats from the very comfortable café. With plenty of homemade food (and the cakes are out of this world), ice creams and best of all the speciality, home reared Wild Boar meat, you'll be spoilt for choice. Why not try some today?

Souvenirs
A small gift shop concludes your visit, where you can purchase a range of 'boar' related memorabilia including some sausages or steaks to take home for the barbeque!

Prices:
Adults £4.50
Children (under 2 FREE) £4.00
O.A.P.'s £4.00

```
picture of wild boars
```

Bowland Wild Boar Park - why 'sty' at home when you can wallow around our park at your leisure!

Examiner comment 1

Grade C:

_____

_____

_____

_____

_____

Examiner comment 2

Grade A:

_____

_____

_____

_____

_____

RAISE MY GRADE

Skills to raise my grade

Now you have completed this lesson on leaflets, it's time to fill in the RAG table below to see if your confidence has improved.

	R	A	G
I know when I am being asked to produce a leaflet.	○	○	○
I know how to prepare for leaflets (thinking about audience, purpose, format and content).	○	○	○
I understand how to structure a leaflet.	○	○	○
I am confident that I know what to include in a leaflet.	○	○	○
I understand how my work will be assessed.	○	○	○

12 Speeches

Skills to raise my grade

Fill in the RAG table below to show how confident you are in the following areas:

	R	A	G
I know when I am being asked to produce a speech.	○	○	○
I know how to prepare for speeches (thinking about audience, purpose, format and content).	○	○	○
I understand how to structure a speech.	○	○	○
I am confident that I know what to include in a speech.	○	○	○
I understand how my work will be assessed.	○	○	○

A speech or talk is when you address a person or group of people about a given topic or issue. Speeches can be written for a number of different reasons. They might be written to give information, to explain, argue or even to persuade your audience.

If you are asked to write a speech in the exam, you are still being marked on your ability to write and punctuate your work correctly. You must not use any slang or some of the conventions you use when talking socially to your friends.

3 minutes

Activity 1

The elements below make an effective written speech. Sort them into those that are part of **writing** the speech and those that relate to **delivering** the speech by writing them into the table opposite.

- A secure grasp of/appeal to the audience
- Accurate punctuation and spelling
- The ability to engage listeners
- Some humour
- Facts and statistics
- Emphasising the key messages
- Repeating the key ideas
- Pausing in the right places
- Making your views very clear
- Linking the ideas carefully
- Not going off on a tangent about something – your speech must be focused at all times
- Using effective techniques in your writing
- Anecdotal evidence

Writing your speech	Delivering your speech

3 minutes

Activity 2

Read the following list of some features of speeches. Draw lines to match each feature to its definition.

Features of speeches	Definition
Repetition	Questions that do not need answers
Anecdotes	Use of simple jokes to interest the audience
Statistics to back up your ideas	Repeating key words/messages so the reader remembers them
Rhetorical questions	Making sure the tone and words suit the topic (i.e. serious/light-hearted)
Memorable phrases/quotes	Use of figures/percentages/numbers to support your ideas
Humour	Phrases/quotes for the audience to remember
Controversial statements	Short stories that are linked to the speech
An appropriate tone to suit the audience	Comments that are deliberately intended to provoke a reaction

Read the transcript for the following interview question and answer.

> Interviewer: You have applied for a job in our nursery. What experience have you got working with young people?
>
> Candidate: Well, erm, I dunno really. I guess I like being with young people because I am still pretty young myself. I'm only 18 and think that I am good for a laugh. I erm, think that, well, erm I get on with people. All my mates think I am sociable and my little brother thinks I am a really cool big brother. I think I will erm like reading to them and playing games with them. Erm, I can't really think of anything else to say.

1 What makes this speech unsuccessful? You might like to think about:
- coherence
- length
- detail
- relevance to task
- sentence structures
- fluency.

_____
_____
_____
_____
_____
_____
_____
_____
_____
_____
_____
_____
_____
_____
_____

25 minutes

When writing a speech it is important that you begin by addressing your audience in an appropriate way and informing them who you are. You should then include a brief introduction where you clarify what your speech will be about.

The next three to four paragraphs will develop your ideas. You should then conclude your speech with a clear summary of your views, and an indication of what may happen next.

Read the following exam question and think about what you might include in an answer.

Could you survive without a mobile phone, computer, TV or games console?'

Write a lively speech for your classmates, giving your views on the advantages or disadvantages of using technology in our everyday lives. *(20 marks)*

The first thing you need to do is to think about the **format** of your speech.

A suggested structure for the format of your speech is included on page 92, with some advice about what you should include at each stage.

1 Use the planning space on page 92 to write down what you will include in each section to answer the exam question above.

2 Read the assessment checklist below and then write an answer to this question, using the space on page 93 and additional paper as necessary. Use the checklist to refer to as you work, aiming to meet as many of the criteria as you can to achieve the best possible grade.

Assessment checklist

Grade C checklist	✓ or ✗
I have identified the correct audience and directed my speech towards them	
I have used a lively but informative tone	
I have arranged my writing into paragraphs	
I have mentioned some of the features from the task	
My ideas are clear and I have added detail	
I have varied the beginnings of some sentences	
My spelling is mostly accurate	
My punctuation is varied and mostly accurate	

Grade A checklist	✓ or ✗
I have deliberately appealed to and engaged my audience	
My format and structure are effective	
I have crafted my tone/language for the audience	
My paragraphs are varied in length and structure	
My writing has detail and is well developed	
I effectively vary sentences throughout	
My spelling is correct	
My vocabulary is varied, effective and extended	
My punctuation is varied and effective	
My tone and overall explanation are very convincing	

Format of a speech	Speech plan
Address • Make sure you address the audience • Think about who you are speaking to as this will guide your formality • Keep it short	
First paragraph • Give a brief outline of the subject you are talking about • Keep this section to a few initial ideas • Make it clear whether you are talking about advantages OR disadvantages	
Main body of the speech • write at least two paragraphs for the main content • Give your opinions • Make each paragraph relevant to the subject or the title of the article • Add plenty of detail so your reader fully understands you • Answer the important questions like 'why', 'how' and 'what' in this section	
Conclusion of the speech • Give a summary of your ideas • Give recommendations/an overview and think about how you will end. Will you end on a question, a fact, an exaggerated sentence, a plea?	

(blank lined writing space)

10 minutes

Activity 5

You will now be given the opportunity to review and assess your work.

1 In the exam it is important to make sure your writing is as accurate as possible. Go back through your work. If there are any spellings that you are unsure of, replace them with something you are more certain of.

2 Highlight all of the punctuation you have used. Use a different colour for each punctuation mark. This will give you a quick visual guide to see if you have varied your punctuation and if you have used enough full stops in your work.

3 Now reflect on your work using the assessment checklist in Activity 4 on page 91. Tick the criteria you feel you have achieved.

Read the exam question below.

> **Write a speech for the Parents' Association at your school, informing them about what it is like being a teenager today.** *(20 marks)*

One of these speeches was awarded a grade C and the other was awarded a grade A. In the space under each of the speeches, write down the grade you think they should be awarded and two or three sentences to explain your reasons. You may want to remind yourself of the Assessment checklist from Activity 4 (page 91) as you consider the grades.

Student 1

Dear Parents,

I am here today to talk to you about what it is like to be a teenager who is living in the year 2011. I hope that you will think my speech gives you a good idea of what is going through the heads of all teenagers and that includes your very own children.

Most people think that many teenagers today have it really easy compared to their parents. People think that we have more money, more possetions and are far more spoilt than our parents but what most people don't realise is that the pressures teenagers are under today are more than our parents had to have. There are less jobs for people leaving school at 16 and that means we have to go to college to get a job which puts us under pressure to do better at school because most parents expect their kids to do better than them.

Some teenagers today get a massive allowance from their parents and are bought the best designer clothes but most of us don't. We have to get jobs and save all of our money just to keep up with the trends and to avoid being bullied. There's a lot of pressure on people today to wear the right clothes, to have the right phone and to even live in the right places. And that pressure is often hard.

Many parents and people in the community have a really bad impression of teenagers as drunken, sex mad and drugged up idiots who run around the streets causing hell. A few teenagers do fit this picture but they are a small group of teenagers causing kayos. Most of us work hard, go out sometimes and have rules to follow at home that give us trouble if they are broken.

It's hard being teenagers so just give us support and space to learn the important lessons we need to know in our own time.

Examiner comment 1

Reasons for grade: _____

_____

_____

_____

_____

Student 2

Drunken, drug taking sex maniacs. This is the picture painted of teenagers by many of the daily tabloids every week. 'Teenage crime on the increase…teen pregnancy crisis…hoodies causing havoc…' The headlines certainly paint a particularly grim picture of my classmates and I. But stop, before you phone the police, do you honestly think we all fit this depressing stereotype?

Look around you. 75% of the students in this school gained 5 A*–grade Cs last year. Isn't that something we can be proud of? Do the headlines mention the 20% increased pass rate at our school? No, they only mention the one idiot who set off a smoke alarm in a local home for the elderly.

Teenagers have it easy according to the older generations. But do any of you really understand the pressures placed upon today's youth? Driven to reach the ever increasing exam statistics and driven to despair by competitive parents who feel we ought to be better than ever. Life as a teen is a tough old ask. And do we complain? Of course we do, but didn't you?

Parents, ask yourself the following question…when you were our age was it important to wear the right clothes, to meet the right boy or girl and to go to the right social events? Of course it was. Only now it all costs that little bit more. We have to get the right clothes and mobile or we're bullied and we even have to have the right parents. Yes, you heard me right, the right parents can mean the difference between fitting in and being totally alienated. So next time you think about embarrassing your child in front on their mates, think again. You're not being cool, you're not being tough, you're just signing a 'right to bully' warrant for your dearly beloved child. Being a teenager is tough – so come on parents – help us out.

Examiner comment 2

Reasons for grade: _____

_____

_____

_____

Skills to raise my grade

Now you have completed this lesson on speeches, it's time to fill in the RAG table below to see if your confidence has improved.

	R	A	G
I know when I am being asked to produce a speech.	○	○	○
I know how to prepare for speeches (thinking about audience, purpose, format and content).	○	○	○
I understand how to structure a speech.	○	○	○
I am confident that I know what to include in a speech.	○	○	○
I understand how my work will be assessed.	○	○	○

13 Reviews

Skills to raise my grade

Fill in the RAG table below to show how confident you are in the following areas:	R	A	G
I know when I am being asked to produce a review.	○	○	○
I know how to prepare for reviews (thinking about audience, purpose, format and content).	○	○	○
I understand how to structure a review.	○	○	○
I am confident that I know what to include in a review.	○	○	○
I understand how my work will be assessed.	○	○	○

Many of us quickly form opinions about the things we watch, read or listen to. Some people like to offer their views in the shape of reviews and these can be very useful when choosing to watch, listen to or buy something.

When producing a review it is important that you give your views and opinions, as well as telling the reader some information about the thing you are reviewing. Getting the right balance is essential – you want a good mix of opinion and information.

5 minutes

Activity 1

1   Which of these definitions is the correct definition of a review? Add a tick.

A review is about the negative points of a product where the writer tells you what is negative about it and why you should not buy something.	
A review is a formal piece of writing that gives you instructions on how to use something.	
A review is usually a written article (but can be spoken, for example a film review on the radio), that gives an *opinion* about something that the writer has listened to, used, seen or read.	

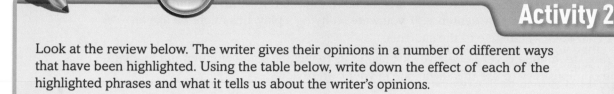

Activity 2

5 minutes

Look at the review below. The writer gives their opinions in a number of different ways that have been highlighted. Using the table below, write down the effect of each of the highlighted phrases and what it tells us about the writer's opinions.

> This film is all about the transformation of cruel bully, Eva Jones, teen heartthrob Kristen Stewart, to an intimidated victim of a huge bullying hoax. And let's be honest, with a storyline like that, it was never going to hit the box office. 'High School Revenge' however is worse than you can imagine. It seriously has to be one of the worst films ever made (and yes, that does include Bob the Builder's Christmas Workout). Admittedly the film is not without its strengths – the scenery is realistic and the special effects are special – but these are not enough to carry what can only be described as the flop of the decade.

Writer's opinion	What is the effect?	What does it tell us about their opinion?
teen heartthrob, Kristen Stewart		
(and yes, that does include Bob the Builder's Christmas Workout)		
the scenery is realistic and the special effects are special		

Each of the highlighted sections on the review gives us an example of parenthesis. Parenthesis is a phrase that is inserted into a sentence to include extra information or an opinion. It is not always directly connected to the sentence. If you were studying a play, this might be like an aside that a character would give to the audience.

This 'top grade' technique is very effective as it allows us to include some humour and to give some subtle opinions. Try to use this technique in your own reviews.

3 minutes

Activity 3

It is important to think about the vocabulary we use when reviewing something. Look at the lists of words below and write (P) or (N) beside each word, according to whether you feel it is positive or negative.

	Positive or negative?		Positive or negative?
Monotonous		Frustrating	
Dated		Enthralling	
Cheap		Woeful	
Engaging		Wooden	
Disappointing		Mesmerising	
Awesome		Accomplished	
Entertaining		Novel	
Flawless		Vibrant	
Dismal		Droll	
Unconvincing		Compelling	
Hollow		Inspiring	
Flat		Tedious	

You can use these words in your own reviews. Make sure you look up any that you don't understand.

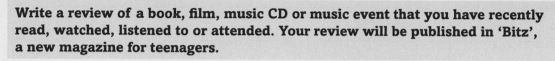

30 minutes

Activity 4

Write a review of a book, film, music CD or music event that you have recently read, watched, listened to or attended. Your review will be published in 'Bitz', a new magazine for teenagers.

(20 marks)

Complete the following planning exercise in response to the exam question above.

Audience _____   Purpose _____

Format _____

Content (what you will include) _____

_____

_____

Read the assessment checklist below and then write an answer to the exam question, using the space on page 100 and continuing on a separate sheet as necessary. Refer to the checklist as you work, aiming to meet as many of the criteria as you can to achieve the best possible grade.

Assessment checklist

Grade C checklist	✓ or ✗
I have identified the correct audience and directed my review towards them	
I have used a lively but informative tone	
I have arranged my writing into paragraphs	
I have given a balance of opinions and details	
My ideas are clear and I have added detail	
I have varied the beginnings of some sentences	
My spelling is mostly accurate	
My punctuation is varied and mostly accurate	

Grade A checklist	✓ or ✗
I have deliberately appealed to and engaged my audience	
My format and structure are effective	
I have crafted my tone/language for the audience	
My paragraphs are varied in length and structure	
My writing has detail and is well developed	
I effectively vary sentences throughout	
My spelling is correct	
My vocabulary is varied, effective and extended	
My punctuation is varied and effective	
My tone and overall explanation are very convincing	

_____
_____
_____
_____

5 minutes

Activity 5

1 Read through the first paragraph of your review from Activity 4 and answer the following success criteria questions.

	✓ or ✗
Is it clear whether your review is about a book, film, music CD or music event?	
Have you included the title/name of the book, film, music, CD or music event?	
Have you made it clear how you feel about the book, film, music CD or music event?	
Do you think the first paragraph is interesting enough to make the reader want to read the rest of your review?	

2 Based on your answers to the questions above, make any changes you think are necessary to improve your review in the space below.

_____
_____
_____
_____

3 Now mark your work in full. Use the tick or cross column beside the Assessment checklist in Activity 4 to mark down your decisions.

4 Write down three tips for how you can improve next time.

- _____
- _____
- _____

GradeStudio

10 minutes

Read the following exam question.

> Write a review of your most memorable book, film, music CD or music
> event of the year.
>
> *(20 marks)*

Read the following extracts from three student reviews, each written to answer the exam question above,
then answer the questions on page 103.

Student 1

Toy Story 3

Does it take us to infinity and beyond?

Pixar's latest (and in my opinion, finest) animated feature film continues the story of Woody, Buzz and
the toys. Andy is now 17 and about to set out for college, prompting his mum to drop off his old toys at
Sunnydale day-care centre. Though sad to leave Andy, the toys are looking forward to a fun filled wonderland
where they'll be played with all day long. Instead they find toy-hell on earth…

The story is a straightforward kids' film at heart but the suspense, laugh out loud humour and super
charged action will send even the most critical (and older) viewer to film heaven.

Student 2

Monster Ball

My expectations were high before heading out to see the one and only Lady Gaga's Monster Ball last night
and with her own unique, quirky and out of this world showmanship, she totally blew any expectations away.
The concert takes you on a wild journey with *Gaga* to find the Monster Ball, the greatest party there ever
was! The journey is crammed with all of our favourite Gaga songs, provocative dance moves, blood-stained
costumes, burning pianos, and even a dress made from what can only be described as metal fans! Love her
or hate her, the sheer sight of the very talented Gaga on stage in nothing more than a bejewelled bikini one
moment and being vomited on with blue paint the next is certainly one for the memory books!

Student 3

The Short Second Life of Bree Tanner

Stephenie Meyer, author of the highly celebrated *Twilight* novels, has had fans eagerly awaiting the latest
instalment. The question on everyone's lips is has she managed to exceed her original if somewhat mediocre
tales? In my opinion, she has not. In the introduction to *The Short Second Life of Bree Tanner*, she caused a
surge of anticipation by suggesting that in this novel she has 'stepped into the shoes of … a 'real' vampire
– a hunter, a monster'. Any readers frustrated by the mundane events in the *Twilight* books – vampires who
play baseball, drive Volvos and give each other kind and thoughtful gifts – might be tempted to perk up.
Sadly, it's a fruitless hope.

Meyer's extraordinary weakness is that she can't bear any of her characters to have grim pasts or less than
acceptable morals. We're promised an untamed, unethical, teenage protagonist, but what we get is Bree…

1 Which introduction do you like best, and why?

_____

_____

2 Which introduction is most effective, and why?

_____

_____

3 Do any of the reviews make you want to buy, watch, read or attend the item/event from the review? Explain why/why not.

_____

_____

4 Imagine you are the examiner. Write a comment about each review, using the assessment checklist in Activity 4, page 99 to guide your judgement.

Student 1: _____

_____

_____

Student 2: _____

_____

_____

Student 3: _____

_____

_____

5 Read the following review and find five words or phrases that you feel are effective. List each of them in the table provided after the review and explain why you think they are effective.

Student 4

'Gleeming' over Glee…

For those of you unfamiliar with Glee, it brings us a combination of all the teenage movies you love to hate. It's 'Bring It On' meets 'High School Musical,' or even 'Pretty in Pink' meets 'Dream Girls.' Before we even switch on our TVs we have formed an opinion, we want to loathe this prefabricated and utterly predictable teenage offering. But… We switch on the TV and see the gleeks gleeming at us with their oh-so uncool (that they become a fashion statement) wardrobes and their incredibly predictable jokes (that leave us rolling off the sofa) and within the blink of an eye, we're hooked.

Glee has captured something, something that so many of us long for. It captures the spirit of X Factor (where thousands of young people long to catch a glimmer of fame and life on the bright side). It captures our sense of competition, our obsession with music (who doesn't sing in the shower?) and has touched the ambition of every teenager who longs for a better life. 'Glee' captures this obsession but it also subtly manages to show us the reality of these dreams.

The episodes follow a predictable pattern but also allow us to see another side to all teens. In the next series we will see the handsome star quarterback, Finn Hudson (Cory Monteith), who secretly loves to sing. We will see him battle with his dreams of a different life but also his fear of rejection by the cool kids if he decides to join the glee club (which is small and made up of unpopular, unattractive misfits). It is these difficult emotional choices which are so real to the rest of us that have allowed Glee to blossom into the cult show that it is today.

'Glee' manages the balance between humour and reality so very well. It has a strong satirical pulse that doesn't weaken the characters' identities or dim the showmanship of a talented cast. Without giving too much away, the cast are predictable too, from the quiet Asian girl to the teacher who loves his work (but whose wife wants him to retrain as an accountant to earn more money). But it is their neediness, their vulnerability and their determination that makes us love them more.

Glee is one of the best new series on TV today. It's a heady mix of quirky, sweet, witty and utterly predictable feel good fun.

Examiner comment

From beginning to end the quality of this review is most impressive. The punctuation is effortlessly effective, and the use of word play and puns is extremely sophisticated. A joy to read!

Effective words/phrases	Reason why this is effective

6 Read the review again and underline in one colour where the writer gives their opinion and in another colour where they give the facts. This will give you a visual record on the balance of fact and opinion needed in a review.

7 What does Student 4 think about Glee?

_____

_____

_____

_____

_____

_____

_____

_____

_____

_____

_____

_____

Skills to raise my grade

RAISE MY GRADE

Now you have completed this lesson on review writing, it's time to fill in the RAG table below to see if your confidence has improved.

	R	A	G
I know when I am being asked to produce a review.	◯	◯	◯
I know how to prepare for reviews (thinking about audience, purpose, format and content).	◯	◯	◯
I understand how to structure a review.	◯	◯	◯
I am confident that I know what to include in a review.	◯	◯	◯
I understand how my work will be assessed.	◯	◯	◯

Do you remember filling in this checklist at the beginning of your revision?

How confident do you feel about each of the areas below that you need to revise for your exam now that you have revised?

Fill in the revision checklist below.

▶ Tick green if you feel confident about this topic.

▶ Tick amber if you know some things, but revision will help improve your knowledge and skills to the best they can be.

▶ Tick red if you are not confident about two or more aspects of this topic.

Remember to ask your teacher for help if you are unsure of any area.

Unit 1: Reading non-fiction texts	R	A	G
1 Locating and retrieving information	○	○	○
2 Impressions	○	○	○
3 Viewpoint and attitude	○	○	○
4 Intended audience	○	○	○
5 Analysis of persuasive techniques	○	○	○
6 Comparison and evaluation of texts	○	○	○
Unit 2: Writing information and ideas			
7 Informal letters	○	○	○
8 Formal letters	○	○	○
9 Reports	○	○	○
10 Articles	○	○	○
11 Leaflets	○	○	○
12 Speeches	○	○	○
13 Reviews	○	○	○

RAISE MY GRADE

If you are still unsure about a few areas, don't worry. You still have time to ask your teacher for help and advice.

What your GCSE exam paper looks like

GCSE

English Language
Higher Tier

Unit 1: Reading non-fiction texts

1 hour

ADDITIONAL MATERIALS

A 12-page answer booklet

Resource Material

INSTRUCTIONS TO CANDIDATES

Answer **all** questions.

Write your answers in the separate answer book provided.

INFORMATION FOR CANDIDATES

The number of marks is given in brackets at the end of each question or part-question.

Reading Paper

The front cover will always remind you how long you have to complete the whole paper (1 hour). You must decide how best to divide up your time in order to read the material carefully and answer all of the questions.

Ideally you should spend about 12 minutes reading all the material very carefully and making any notes you think may help you to answer the questions.

You should then aim to spend 12 minutes answering each question. Remember to focus on the correct area of the text and underline the key words in the question.

Remember to answer all the questions on the paper and read through your answers carefully before the end of the exam.

For English, these papers will be called 'English in the Daily World'.

English Language
Higher Tier

Unit 2: Writing information and ideas

1 hour

Writing Paper

The front cover will always remind you how long you have to complete the whole paper (1 hour). It will always suggest that you divide your time equally between the two questions (about 30 minutes on each question).

Check your answers carefully before the end of the exam because 7 marks on each question are given for sentence structure, punctuation and spelling.

Remember to answer both the questions and aim to write about one and a half sides in your answer booklet for each question.

ADDITIONAL MATERIALS

A 12-page answer booklet

Resource Material

INSTRUCTIONS TO CANDIDATES

Answer **all** questions.

Write your answers in the separate answer book provided.

You are advised to spend your time as follows:
Q.1 – about 30 minutes
Q.2 – about 30 minutes

INFORMATION FOR CANDIDATES

The number of marks is given in brackets at the end of each question or part-question.

Reading paper Unit 1

*Answer **all** the following questions.*

***The Resource Material** is an extract from an article by Ernest Dodds 'Should we Bemoan the Mobile Phone?' which appeared on a parents' Internet forum page.*

The second text is a fact sheet 'Back to basics: choosing a mobile phone', based on an article by Clive Woodyear which appeared in the Sunday Times.

Look at Text 1, the 'Should we Bemoan the Mobile Phone?' article.

1. Look at the first part of the article on the opposite page. How does Ernest Dodds feel that mobile phones can help us in everyday life?

   10 marks

2. Now look at the rest of the article. What are the writer's thoughts and feelings about mobile phones?

   10 marks

Now look at Text 2, the 'Back to basics: choosing a mobile phone' fact sheet.

3. How does the fact sheet aim to help the reader when they are choosing a mobile phone?

   10 marks

You should now use details and information <u>from both texts</u> to answer the following question:

4. Compare and contrast the two texts and what the writers say about mobile phones.

   You should organise your answer into two paragraphs using the following headings:

   - the advantages of mobile phones;
   - the effects of mobile phones on our lives.

   10 marks

Text 1

Should we Bemoan the Mobile Phone?

Ernest Dodds

According to a recent poll, almost 50% of teenagers believe the mobile phone is one of the most useful inventions of the last century. People, it would seem, just can't live without them. Despite the fact that 1.7 billion people throughout the world live in poverty, 6 out of 10 people in the world own a mobile phone and that number is increasing at an alarming daily rate.

The benefits of a mobile phone are undeniable. Not only are they portable, so you never have to miss any calls, but you can use them in extreme situations to call for emergency services. Yes, I do realise that countless lives must have been saved due to mobile phones, not to mention jobs saved when running late for important meetings, but how many of us really need to use the phonebook on a regular basis, or the calculator, or for that matter, the camera (yet again useful in an accident though). My daughter claims they are great if you get lost as you can surf or ring for directions. I say, learn how to read a map or ask for directions. I appreciate that texting can be useful as can the musical features too. But I just don't understand why we have to let them rule our lives.

I get the benefits, I really do, but at the back of my mind there is still a nagging doubt. Of course I own one; I use it and can see its value. For example, only last week my teenage daughter missed a bus and after a quick text I was able to collect her and have complete peace of mind about her safety. My wife claims she feels more relaxed knowing that our children carry phones with them to school and when they are out on an evening. But while they have become almost surgically attached to most members of our household, I'll admit it, I do still feel some concerns about the very limited research into the safety of mobile technology.

Let's think about it … less than 100 years ago we were handing out cigarettes to troops on the front line. Now we're told to avoid being in the same street as another smoker for fear of being affected by passive smoking. Do the phones transmit harmful rays, however small? Do the headsets cause damage to the body or brain? I don't know the answers but the questions still worry me.

Alongside any potential physical threats, what concerns me more are the social effects of mobile phones. Yesterday I embarked on a train journey from Glasgow to Manchester and was horrified by what I saw. Quite honestly, no one spoke. No one even looked up in my carriage for more than one minute as they were too busy texting, emailing, working and chatting on their phones. I asked the young man who was sitting next to me to kindly turn down the music blaring out of his phone headset and you would have thought I'd asked him to walk to Manchester. We seem to be hiding behind our phones and this is only making us more and more anti-social.

The disadvantages are far-reaching and a few examples are listed below:

- cheating in quizzes, exams and tests
- increased buying
- theft of expensive phones
- competition and pressure about the 'best phones'
- they can damage the ear.

My daughter never talks to her friends; it's all MSM, texting and twittering. She doesn't go out a great deal either, claiming that she keeps in touch online on her iPhone.

Do I think we should ban the phone? No, of course we shouldn't. But, like cigarettes, we should ban their use in certain places and more importantly learn to live without them once in a while.

Text 2

Back to basics: choosing a mobile phone

So where do you start if you just want a basic, easy-to-use handset?

Before you start searching for models, take a little time to consider what you need. First, think about what **style** of phone you want. Models fall into categories such as candybar-shaped, slider (which offers protection for the keypad and camera lens), clamshell (also called flip-phones), Qwerty phones with a keypad (useful for texting) and the increasingly popular touchscreen type. Although popular, touchscreen models can be difficult to read in bright sunlight and vary considerably in their ease-of-use.

Think about the features you need. If you want a basic mobile phone, **ease of making a voice call** should top your list of priorities. Good-sized buttons will help here, as will a simple menu system that will enable you to recall the telephone numbers for your favourite contacts.

Texting

After voice calls, **texting** is an important feature to consider. It is an increasingly popular way of keeping in touch, particularly with teenagers! An astonishing 4.1 million text messages are sent on average every hour in Britain. All phones, with the exception of just a few specialist models, can send and receive text messages. If texting is of prime importance, choose a phone with well-spaced buttons that feel comfortable to use. A Qwerty keypad can make texting easier.

Does size matter?

A good quality and reasonable-sized screen makes sense. Check the size of the text and numbers on the screen. Some cheap phones have a tiny screen text that anyone with less than perfect vision will struggle to read. Look for a phone with a colour screen with a good resolution. Screen resolution is expressed in the number of pixels – most new mid- to high-end mobile phones have at least 240 x 320 pixel resolution.

What other features are on offer?

Even the most basic of phones will offer a wide range of features such as **alarms**, **timers** and a **calendar**. A camera and the ability to play music are features that are now available on many basic phones. Using a **camera** to take a quick snap can be fun and, although the image quality won't be as good as that of a good quality digital camera, you're more likely to have your phone when a photo opportunity arises.

Listening to **music** on mobile phones is very popular, and saves carrying around a separate MP3 player or radio. If this is of interest, it makes sense if your chosen phone supports the same music format as you use on your computer. You also need to think about battery life. Infrequent users are far more likely to find their phone has a flat battery when they finally want to use it. Regular users usually charge their phone every day or two as a matter of routine. Phones vary considerably in how long their batteries last, but take some of the manufacturers' more extravagant standby and talk-time claims with a 'pinch of salt'!

And finally…

Finally, although it might seem obvious, before you choose any phone tied to a network or a contract, make sure that you will get a **signal** in the main areas where you plan to use it. Networks vary considerably in their coverage of the country, particularly in rural and remote areas. If you are not sure, ask friends, family, or work colleagues which network provides good signal coverage for them. Don't just rely on the predictions made by the networks!

Writing paper Unit 2

*Answer Question 1 **and** Question 2.*

In this section you will be assessed for your writing skills, including the presentation of your work. Take special care with handwriting, spelling, punctuation and layout.

Think about the purpose, audience and, where appropriate, the format for your writing.

A guide to the amount you should write is given at the end of each question.

1. A day in the life of…

    You have been asked to write a lively article for a magazine, discussing the use of technology (computers, mobile phones, etc.) in a typical teenager's day.   20 marks

    The quality of your writing is more important than its length. You should write about one to two pages in your answer book.

2. You have been involved in a recycling and energy-saving project at school.

    As part of your project, you have to give a talk to teachers at the school with the title 'How to live a Greener Life'.

    Write what you would say.   20 marks

    The quality of your writing is more important than its length. You should write about one to two pages in your answer book.

Personal notes and reminders

You may want to use this page to write down your personal revision targets, as well as any useful hints and tips you have learnt during your revision lessons to make your revision successful.